ATLAS OF HISTORY'S GREATEST

MILITARY VICTORIES

THE 50 MOST SIGNIFICANT MOMENTS EXPLORED IN WORDS AND MAPS

Jeremy Harwood

ATLAS OF HISTORY'S GREATEST

MILITARY VICTORIES

THE 50 MOST SIGNIFICANT MOMENTS EXPLORED IN WORDS AND MAPS

Jeremy Harwood

Published in the UK in 2013 by
Icon Books Ltd, Omnibus Business Centre,
39–41 North Road, London N7 9DP
email: info@iconbooks.net
www.iconbooks.net

Sold in the UK and Europe
by Faber & Faber Ltd, Bloomsbury House,
74–77 Great Russell Street,
London WC1B 3DA or their agents

Distributed in the UK and Europe
by TBS Ltd, TBS Distribution Centre, Colchester Road,
Frating Green, Colchester CO7 7DW

Published in Australia in 2013 by Allen & Unwin Pty Ltd,
PO Box 8500, 83 Alexander Street,
Crows Nest, NSW 2065

ISBN: 978-184831578-5

This book was produced by
Quantum Books
6 Blundell Street
London N7 9BH

Publisher: Sarah Bloxham

Managing Editor: Samantha Warrington

Project Editor: Marilyn Inglis

Assistant Editor: Jo Morley

Copy Editor: Robin Buckland

Editorial Intern: Rebecca Cave

Production Manager: Rohana Yusof

Design: Andrew Easton, www.ummagummacreative.co.uk

Cartographer: Red Lion Mapping

Printed in Hong Kong by Hung Hing

Contents

Introduction

WARFARE HAS BEEN A CONSTANT OF HUMAN HISTORY SINCE EARLIEST TIMES. THIS AUTHORITATIVE ATLAS SINGLES OUT 50 OF THE GREATEST MILITARY VICTORIES AND DEFEATS OF ALL TIME, EXPLAINING WHY AND HOW THEY WERE FOUGHT AND ALSO REVEALING WHAT MAKES THEM SO HIGHLY SIGNIFICANT.

War has been part of human history ever since *Homo sapiens* first emerged and started to dominate the planet. In prehistoric times, a state of what today would be called guerrilla warfare was probably endemic; as civilized societies gradually came into existence, war became more organized and intensive as nation-states and then empires battled each other for supremacy. Indeed, war, social and historical change have always been closely associated, as any study of history shows.

The verdict of war, so it would seem, has been a key factor in deciding the course of historical evolution from ancient times onwards. In Classical days, the Greek victory in the Persian Wars saved western Europe from coming under an Asiatic dictatorship, while Charles Martel's defeat of the Moors at the battle of Tours was decisive in halting further Muslim expansion into Europe, at least until

the coming of the Ottoman Turks many centuries later. It is also true to say that the rise and fall of almost all the great empires of history has been associated with military success or failure. War, it seems, has always been the ultimate arbiter of human destiny.

It is also clear that warfare, as Thomas Hardy said in *The Dynasts*, makes 'rattling good history'. In the same book, he opined that 'Peace is poor reading'. For his part, the great Prussian military philosopher Carl von Clausewitz described it as a 'passionate drama' at much the same time as he was defining it somewhat more cynically as 'a mere continuation of policy by other means'. Historically, few other subjects possess as much tension, excitement and unpredictability. Despite its grimness, it possesses an eternal fascination all of its own.

Through its close analysis of 50 of the most significant military victories and defeats in world history, this atlas reveals how the art and science of warfare have developed from the time of the ancient Greeks up to the present day. It demonstrates, too, what can be learned from a close study of past battles and campaigns. Napoleon drew on his knowledge of the Punic Wars when he led his army over the Alps into Italy in spring 1800. The Austrians believed the feat impossible, but Napoleon was fully aware that Hannibal and his war elephants had accomplished it. It also shows what can happen when the lessons of the past are ignored. Napoleon and Hitler both failed to learn from the example of Charles XII of Sweden when he undertook a similar enterprise in 1709 and, in the end, both their invasions of Russia ended in a similar catastrophe.

It is, however, deceptive, if not downright dangerous, to look on war as an isolated phenomenon. According to von Clausewitz, it is impossible to understand the significance of any particular battle – let alone an entire war – without taking into account the political circumstances that lie behind any such confrontation. Even this, many military historians have argued, is not enough. It is equally important, they say, to take into account the relationships between governments and their armies, the military theories currently in vogue and their origins, the types of weapons employed, the general state of technological development and the actual methods of fighting available at the time. Terrain, climate and weather must also be taken into full account.

So, too, should the characteristics of the individuals involved. Often, the greatest victories have turned on seemingly minute incidents – 'the single drop of water' as Napoleon wrote, 'that causes the bucket to flow over'. There are some things, however, that have always been unpredictable. It was also Napoleon who said that all successful generals possessed one quality that outranked all others. When asked what that quality was, he simply replied: 'luck'.

ANCIENT WORLD

Warfare in the ancient world revolved around the Middle East and the Mediterranean, where various great powers fought at different times to establish their dominance. The Greeks, led by Alexander the Great, dominated the region for some time, until the Romans eventually triumphed.

Battle of Marathon

THE ATHENIAN DEFEAT OF THE PERSIAN INVADERS AT MARATHON IN 490 BC IS
ONE OF THE KEY BATTLES OF EARLY HISTORY. THE VICTORY ENSURED THAT THE
GREEK CITY-STATES AVOIDED FOREIGN CONQUEST; IT IS THOUGHT TO BE A DEFINING
MOMENT IN THE GROWTH OF WESTERN CIVILIZATION.

When an armada of 600 ships landed a well-equipped force of around 20,000 infantry and cavalry on Greek soil just north of Athens in September 490 BC, practically no one expected anything other than a Persian triumph. Darius I's troops were certainly full of confidence, even though two previous attempts at invasion had been fiascos. Ever since Darius again ordered his forces to attack mainland Greece in reprisal for the support that the Greeks had given to the revolting Ionian city-states in Asia Minor, their progress had been immediate and swift.

The Persians had quickly captured Euboea, a large island off the Attic coast. They knew that Athens, their next target, lacked allies. The Spartans, preoccupied with celebrating a major religious festival,

The Greek generals were at first divided as to what their best course of action was. Some advised waiting in the hope that, after all, reinforcements would arrive...

were unable to come immediately to the Athenians' aid. Although the Plataens had loyally despatched 1,000 warriors to Athens, these could be safely discounted as an insignificant reinforcement. Even with the Plataens, the Athenians could put only around 10,000 men into the field at best. The Persians, therefore, anticipated achieving a decisive victory, which they planned to follow up immediately. While they were slaughtering the Athenian hoplites, their fleet would sail round the coast and attack the city of Athens itself. Without an army to defend it, its citizens would be forced to surrender the city.

THE GENERALS DIFFER

The two armies were to confront one another on the plain of Marathon, some 42 km (26 miles) north of Athens. According

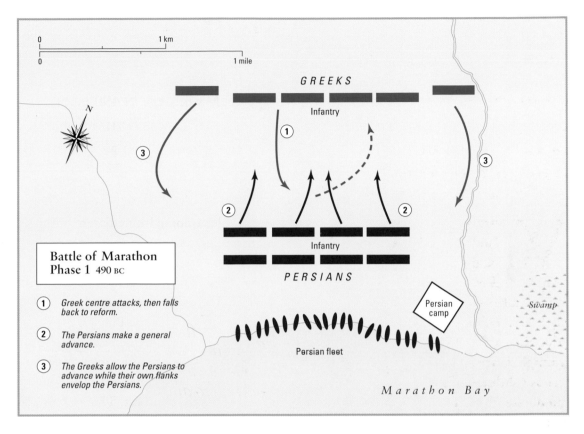

GREEKS

Infantry

PERSIANS

**Battle of Marathon
Phase 1** 490 BC

① Greek centre attacks, then falls back to reform.

② The Persians make a general advance.

③ The Greeks allow the Persians to advance while their own flanks envelop the Persians.

Infantry

Persian camp

Swamp

Persian fleet

Marathon Bay

Phase 1 of the Battle of Marathon, showing the positions the infantry took up on both sides and the initial manoeuvres.

to Herodotus, who wrote his celebrated account of the battle a few years after it was fought, the Greek generals were at first divided as to what their best course of action was. Some advised waiting in the hope that, A all, reinforcements would arrive from Sparta to counter the Persians' numcrical superiority. Others argued for launching an immediate attack. While both sides sat in their respective camps for nine days, each waiting for the other to make the first move, the ten Athenian generals – one from each of the city's tribes – debated before taking a vote. The result was a tie, with five generals voting to wait for the Spartans and five, led by Miltiades, Athens' most brilliant military strategist, in favour of striking first. Miltiades, Herodotus says, then appealed to Callimachus, an Athenian dignitary who enjoyed the honoured position of *polemarch* (war ruler) and held the deciding vote. Miltiades' words were apparently decisive in swaying the dignitary's decision. 'With you it rests, Callimachus', Herodotus reported him as saying, 'either to lead Athens to slavery, or, by securing her freedom, to leave behind to all future generations a memory far beyond that of those who made Athens a democracy. For never since the time the Athenians became a people were they in so great a danger than now.' Callimachus voted in favour of attack.

Miltiades, who now assumed overall command, had a major advantage. He had fought for the Persians for a time and thus had inside knowledge of the battle tactics they customarily employed. He knew, for instance, that they often relied on their cavalry to clinch the victory. Therefore, when he learnt that, for whatever reason, the Persian cavalry was absent from the field, he readied his men for action.

Phase 2 of the Battle of Marathon, illustrating the Greek tactics and the Persian retreat to their ships.

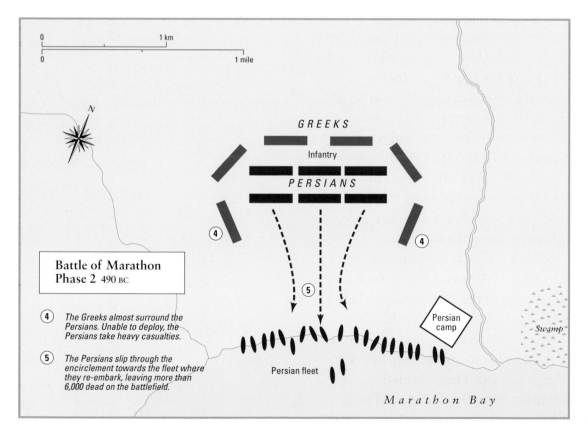

GREEKS

Infantry

PERSIANS

**Battle of Marathon
Phase 2** 490 BC

(4) *The Greeks almost surround the Persians. Unable to deploy, the Persians take heavy casualties.*

(5) *The Persians slip through the encirclement towards the fleet where they re-embark, leaving more than 6,000 dead on the battlefield.*

Persian camp

Swamp

Persian fleet

Marathon Bay

OUTFOXING THE PERSIANS

Miltiades planned the battle carefully. Despite being so heavily outnumbered, he ordered the Athenians to form a battle line equal in length to that of the Persians, but strengthening its two wings at the expense of the centre. Moving at a brisk pace, the Athenians advanced across the plain towards the Persian camp. Miltiades' aim was to get to close quarters as quickly as he could before the Persians could get their archers into action.

In the ensuing melee, the middle of the Athenian line was forced back. The Persians rushed forwards in pursuit, falling neatly into the trap Miltiades had set for them. As they advanced, the two wings of the Athenian army swung forwards and inwards to catch them in what is termed in military parlance a double envelopment. As panic started to spread in their ranks, more and more Persians made for the safety of their ships. The Athenians pursued them to the shore.

Miltiades then force-marched his army back to Athens, arriving there in time to thwart the Persians once again. When their fleet arrived off the city, which the surviving Persians had hoped would be open to attack, they found it fully garrisoned. They were left with no choice but to sail back to Asia. The myth of Persian military invincibility had been shattered forever and many historians believe that the Greek victory at Marathon proved a pivotal point in the history of Western civilization. The legacy of the epic marathon run by Phillippides to bring the news of the victory to Athens lives on in every marathon run that takes place today.

FACT FILE

Battle of Marathon

Date: September 490 BC

Location: Marathon, Greece

Historical Context: The Greco-Persian Wars (492–449 BC)

States Involved: Greece; Persia

Commanders and Leaders: Miltiades the Younger, Callimachus (Athenians); Darius, Artaphernes (Persians)

Outcome: Decisive Greek victory

Aftermath: The Greek victory shattered the myth of Persian military invincibility

Battle of Salamis

WHEN XERXES, DARIUS' ELDEST SON AND SUCCESSOR ON THE PERSIAN THRONE, ATTACKED GREECE IN 480 BC, HE GAVE HIS NAVY A CRUCIAL ROLE TO PLAY IN SUPPORTING HIS INVASION. ITS DEFEAT AT SALAMIS THE SAME YEAR WAS A KEY FACTOR IN ENSURING CONTINUED GREEK SURVIVAL.

Determined to succeed where his father had failed, Xerxes planned his invasion of Greece extremely carefully. As his army pushed south into Thrace and northern Greece, it was supported by a vast naval fleet, which kept pace with Xerxes and his troops as they moved southwards down the coast. The idea was simple. Should the Greeks make a stand against the Persian land forces, the fleet would threaten to land fresh troops in their rear. It also carried the supplies Xerxes and his army needed to fuel their speedy advance.

The Greek strategy was based on one main premise. It was to fight only where the Persians would be unable to take advantage of their numerical supremacy. This was what lay behind the decision to give battle at Thermopylae, the narrow pass

The Greek strategy was based on one main premise. It was to fight only where the Persians would be unable to take advantage of their numerical supremacy.

that was the gateway to southern Greece. Despite the courage of Leonidas, the ruler of Sparta, and his doughty warriors, who, so it was reported, fought to the last man, the Persians won the battle. The road to Athens was open.

The city was hastily evacuated and the army fell back to a new position on the Isthmus of Corinth to defend the Peloponnesus; the fleet, mainly made up of Athenian, Peloponnesian, Isthmian, Euboean and Aeginetan vessels, moved to ports on the island of Salamis. It was vastly outnumbered by the Persian armada, which was 1,200 vessels strong. The Greeks had 380 ships ready for action.

As Persia itself was an inland nation, its fleet was crewed by Phoenicians, Egyptians and Ionian Greeks from Asia Minor. Xerxes did not think the Ionians were totally to be trusted, and so he decided to keep a close personal eye on them in the ensuing battle. Contemporaries record that he watched the action seated on a golden throne, set up at a headland vantage point overlooking Salamis and the intervening strait.

DECEIVING THE PERSIANS
On Salamis itself, the Greek commanders were divided as to what best to do. Some were in favour of sailing to the Isthmus

The Greek ploy to fight within the confines of the islands was a masterful stroke of naval strategy by the Athenian commander Themistocles.

of Corinth to support their compatriots on land. Themistocles, the wily Athenian commander, argued for staying put. He believed that, though smaller, the Greek fleet could neutralize the Persian superiority in numbers if it could fight in the confined waters around the island.

Xerxes originally decided to avoid any such clash. Instead, he began moving troops towards the isthmus, hoping that the Peloponnesians would desert Themistocles and sail to protect their homelands. Then, he received news from

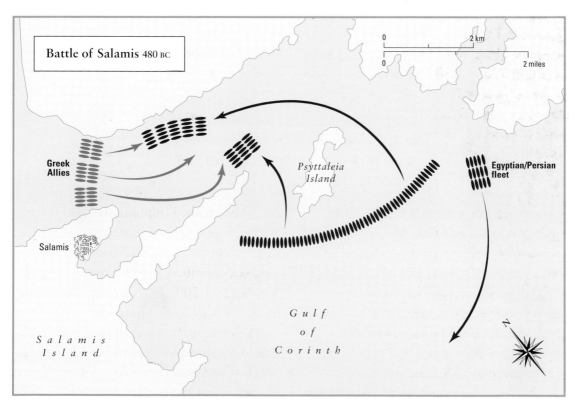

Battle of Salamis 480 BC

A relief of Achaemenid soldiers guarding the Palace of One Hundred Columns at Persepolis, one of the capital cities of the Persian Empire.

a Greek informant that the Athenians themselves wanted to switch sides. The information, of course, was false. It had been supplied by Themistocles, who was anxious not to give his quarrelsome allies the chance to disperse.

The Persian ruler decided to take immediate advantage of this apparent disunity. He ordered the Egyptians to sail around Salamis to block the Straits of Megara to the west and the eastern division of the fleet to do the same to the east. The main body of the fleet was strung out in long lines against the Attic shore. At dawn, it moved forwards to engage the enemy.

AN ATHENIAN TRIUMPH

With the exception of Themistocles, most of the Greek commanders were thrown into confusion by the sudden Persian move. Xerxes' fleet was able to start its attack before they were able to get all their ships underway. However, they swiftly rallied and, before long, a general engagement developed in the narrows. This was just what Themistocles had intended from the start. Indeed, the delay in putting to sea may have worked to the Greeks' advantage, since the Persians, thinking that their foes were attempting to withdraw, began to lose cohesion in their hitherto disciplined ranks.

The Athenians, on the west wing of the Greek fleet, scored the first success. Their superior seamanship helped them to overwhelm the Phoenicians opposing them. Ariabignes, the Phoenicians'

admiral, was killed early in the fighting, leaving them leaderless. The Athenians then turned east to take the Ionians – already locked in battle with the Peloponnesians and Aeginetans – in the flank and rear.

The Persians tried to withdraw, but, as one ship collided with another, the retreat turned into a rout. According to contemporary accounts, 200 of their ships were sunk while the Greeks lost only around 40 vessels. Though the Persians were still numerically superior, Xerxes ordered his battered fleet to sail north to defend the Hellespont.

The victory was a turning point in the Persian Wars. Even more significantly for the future, it marked the emergence of Athens as a great naval power.

FACT FILE

Battle of Salamis

Date: 480 BC

Location: Salamis

Historical Context: The Greco-Persian Wars (492–449 BC)

States Involved: Greece; Persia

Commanders and Leaders: Themistocles, Eurybiades (Greeks); Xerxes I of Persia, Artemisia I of Caria, Ariabignes (Persians)

Outcome: Decisive Greek victory

Aftermath: A turning point in the Greco-Persian Wars; marked the emergence of Athens as a great naval power

Thermopylae

THERMOPYLAE IS REGARDED AS BEING ONE OF THE MOST REMARKABLE BATTLES OF ALL TIME. ALTHOUGH NOT STRICTLY SPEAKING A GREAT VICTORY, THE BRAVERY LEONIDAS AND HIS SPARTANS DISPLAYED BY RESISTING THE PERSIANS IN A FIGHT TO THE DEATH ENSURED THEM MILITARY IMMORTALITY.

The tomb of the great Persian leader Xerxes next to that of Darius the Great, at Naqsh-e Rustam in present day Iran.

It was Themistocles, Athens' most competent commander, who suggested that Thermopylae, a narrow pass with a high cliff on one side and the sea on the other, was the best place for the Greeks to make their initial stand against the invading Persians. In August 480 BC, Leonidas, one of the two kings of Sparta, established a defensive position there. He stationed most of his men behind a wall the Phocians had erected at the narrowest point of the pass. He also despatched 1,000 Phocians to guard a mountain trail that wound its way around and behind his position.

Xerxes held off attacking the Spartans for four days while he unsuccessfully tried to persuade them to surrender. Then his men advanced into the pass. Taking up position in a defensive phalanx in front of the wall, the Spartans drove back wave

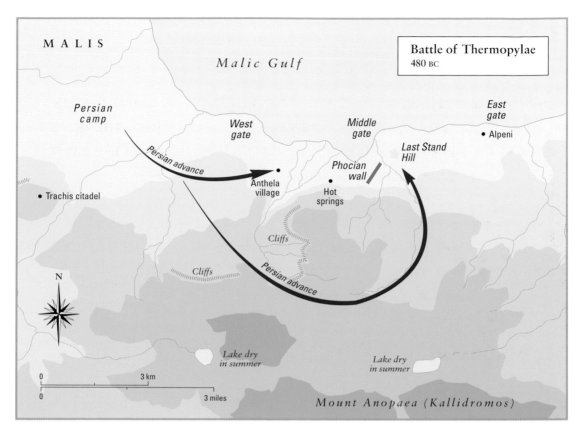

MALIS

Malic Gulf

Battle of Thermopylae
480 BC

Persian
camp

*West
gate*

*Middle
gate*

*East
gate*

• Alpeni

Persian advance

Last Stand
Hill

*Phocian
wall*

• Trachis citadel

Anthela
village

Hot
springs

Cliffs

Cliffs

Persian advance

N

*Lake dry
in summer*

*Lake dry
in summer*

0   3 km

0   3 miles

Mount Anopaea (Kallidromos)

*The Persian advance towards the Phocian Wall during the Battle of
Thermopylae.*

after wave of the Persian attackers. Even
Xerxes' celebrated Immortals failed to
break through the defences.

BETRAYED BY A RENEGADE
As the second day of battle drew to a close,
Ephialtes, a Trachinian turncoat, alerted
Xerxes to the existence of the trail the
Phocians were guarding. The Persian king

promptly ordered a substantial portion of
his army to take the trail and so outflank
the Spartans. Taken by surprise, the
Phocians tried to make a stand against the
Persians, but failed.

Most of the Greeks were in favour of
retreating, but retreat was not a word in
the Spartan vocabulary. The Spartans,
Thespians and Thebans held their ground,
while the rest of the Greeks slipped away.
It was a sound tactical decision. Had
the Spartans retreated, there would have

been nothing to stop the Persian cavalry slaughtering the rest of the army.

Xerxes ordered his troops to attack again. This time, the Spartans moved forward to meet the assault at the widest part of the pass, determined to inflict the maximum number of casualties. Leonidas was killed in the ensuing action. The survivors retired behind the wall to make a last stand.

Retreat was not a word in the Spartan vocabulary. The Spartans, Thespians and Thebans held their ground, while the rest of the Greeks slipped away.

Although the Thebans finally surrendered, the Spartans and Thespians fought to the last man.

Thermopylae was a defeat for the Greeks. However, it won them invaluable time to mobilize fully. Estimates as to the number of casualties vary. Some sources say that 20,000 Persians were slain, though this is almost certainly an exaggeration. Some 2,000 Greeks were killed.

FACT FILE

Thermopylae

Date: August 480 BC

Location: Thermopylae, Greece

Historical Context: The Greco-Persian Wars (492–449 BC)

States Involved: Greece; Persia

Commanders and Leaders: Themistocles, Leonidas I, Demophilus (Greeks); Xerxes I of Persia, Mardonius, Hydarnes (Persians)

Outcome: Persian victory

Aftermath: Despite the Persian victory, the bravery displayed by Leonidas and his Spartans ensured them military immortality

This monument to Leonidas stands at Thermopylae as a testament to the Spartans' bravery and tenacity.

Gaugamela

ONE OF THE MOST DECISIVE BATTLES IN HISTORY, ALEXANDER THE GREAT'S DEFEAT OF DARIUS III OF PERSIA ENDED OVER TWO CENTURIES OF ACHAEMENID RULE AND LED TO THE ESTABLISHMENT OF A NEW, MIGHTY GREEK EMPIRE.

Alexander the Great's attack on the mighty Persian Empire was one of the greatest campaigns in all military history. It started with the defeat of Darius' generals at Granicus on the Hellespont in 334 BC and continued with Alexander's first victory over Darius himself at Issus in Syria the following year. Gaugamela, the battle that was to decide the fate of the Achaemenid Empire, was fought three years later on 1 October 331 BC.

Alexander used the intervening period to consolidate his rule over the lands he had already conquered and to secure the Mediterranean coastline in his rear. Spurning Darius' peace proposals, he turned eastwards again, looking to topple Darius from his throne and so bring the war to a triumphant conclusion. Advancing inland across Mesopotamia, he crossed the rivers Tigris and Euphrates unopposed. Darius, in the meantime, was mobilizing all Persia's vast resources. Both men knew that their next confrontation would be the decisive battle of the war.

Bust of Alexander the Great, who defeated the Persians at the Battle of Gaugamela in 331 BC.

PREPARING FOR BATTLE

It was Darius who chose the battlefield. Desperate to prevent Alexander advancing further into the fertile Mesopotamian heartlands, he mustered his forces on an 11-km (7-mile) plain near the hamlet of Gaugamela, levelling the ground to favour his chariots and planting it with long wooden spikes to deter Alexander's cavalry. He had 16,000 infantry at his disposal – including some mercenary Greek hoplites – 40,000 cavalry and 200 chariots, plus

Phase 1 of the Battle of Gaugamela, illustrating the movements made by the Macedonians and the Persians.

a host of tribesmen from all quarters of his domains. Alexander's invading army consisted of 40,000 infantry and 7,000 cavalry, drawn mainly from Macedonia, Thrace and other parts of Greece. Given the disparity in numbers, the Persian king was confident of victory.

Advancing to within 6 km (4 miles) of the Persian camp, Alexander bivouacked for the night. Having reconnoitred the area, he then conferred with his generals. He turned down the suggestion of a night attack, saying that was exactly what Darius would be expecting. Instead, he moved

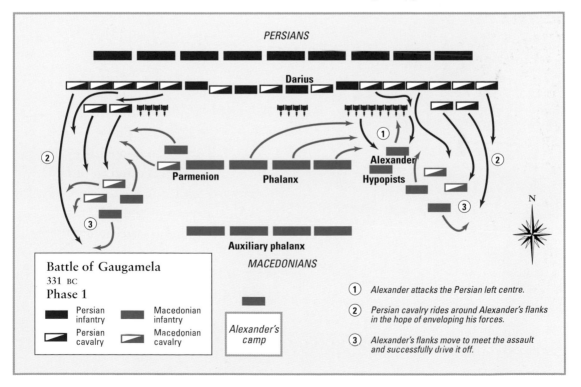

PERSIANS

Darius

②

Alexander
Hypopists

②

Parmenion   Phalanx

③

Auxiliary phalanx
MACEDONIANS

N

Battle of Gaugamela
331 BC
Phase 1

◼ Persian infantry
◼ Macedonian infantry
▨ Persian cavalry
▨ Macedonian cavalry

◼ *Alexander's camp*

① *Alexander attacks the Persian left centre.*

② *Persian cavalry rides around Alexander's flanks in the hope of enveloping his forces.*

③ *Alexander's flanks move to meet the assault and successfully drive it off.*

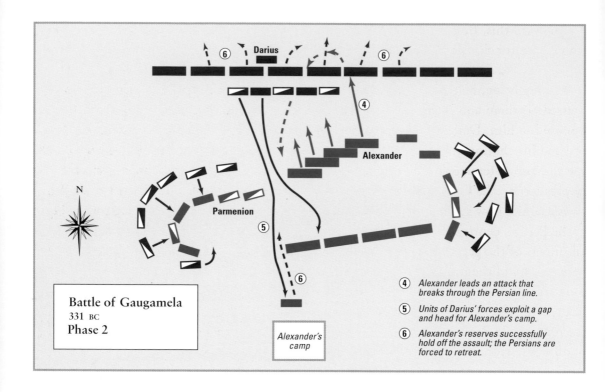

Battle of Gaugamela
331 BC
Phase 2

Alexander's
camp

④ *Alexander leads an attack that
   breaks through the Persian line.*

⑤ *Units of Darius' forces exploit a gap
   and head for Alexander's camp.*

⑥ *Alexander's reserves successfully
   hold off the assault; the Persians are
   forced to retreat.*

*Phase 2 of the Battle of Gaugamela, illustrating the two armies' tactics and
the Persian retreat.*

on the Persian position the next morning,
deploying the bulk of his hoplites in two
central phalanxes, one slightly behind the
other. He himself led the cavalry on the
right wing, while Parmenion, his second-
in-command, took charge of the cavalry
on the left. Both Alexander and Parmenion
were accompanied by light infantry. Darius
deployed the bulk of his infantry in a long
line across the plain, stationing his cavalry
and chariots in front of them.

ALEXANDER STRIKES

All the Greek formations were capable of
acting as independent units – if necessary
in isolation. Alexander started the battle
by ordering his cavalry to move obliquely
towards the extreme right of the plain. This
meant that Bessus, the commander of the
Persian left wing, was obliged to extend his
own line as well to avoid being outflanked
and also preserving the advantage his
superior numbers gave him. However, the
move meant that the Persian centre could
not maintain contact with its left without
being drawn sideways in its turn.

To avoid this, Bessus decided on an immediate attack. Alexander was too quick for Bessus and struck first. In fierce hand-to-hand fighting, he triumphed over the massed Scythian and Bactrian horsemen opposed to him. Darius, meanwhile, ordered his chariots forwards but, despite their fearsome reputation, they made little impression on the Greek phalanxes.

Alexander now swung inwards to strike at the Persian centre's flank, taking full advantage of the gap that had opened between it and the routed Persian left. It soon started to crumble under the weight of the ferocious Greek attack. Darius fled the field, while Bessus, too, fell back in headlong retreat.

The battle was not quite over. Alexander was forced to halt his pursuit of the fleeing Persians to come to the rescue of Parmenion, whose right wing had been forced back by the Persians opposing it and hence had been separated from the rest of the Greek army. The Persian cavalry took advantage of the resulting gap to break through and threaten Parmenion from the rear. Fortunately for him, many of the Persians chose to loot the Greek camp rather than to attack. As Alexander circled back to help Parmenion, he rallied his men and managed to drive the Persians back. They, too, promptly fled. Parmenion went on to attack the Persian camp and loot Darius' baggage train, which fell into Greek hands.

The defeat was a disaster for Darius. Though he managed to reach safety in Ecbatana, Alexander, turning south, captured Babylon, Susa and finally Persepolis, the great Persian capital. It was the end for the Achaemenids – and for Darius himself. Within a year he was dead, murdered by Bessus and other conspiring Persian generals.

FACT FILE
Gaugamela

Date: 1 October 331 BC

Location: A wide plain near Gaugamela

Historical Context: The Greco-Persian Wars (492–449 BC)

States Involved: Macedonia, Greek Allies; Persia

Commanders and Leaders: Alexander the Great, Parmenion, Hephaestion, Craterus, Ptolemy, Antigonus, Seleucus, Perdiccas, Cleitus, Nearchus (Macedonians and Greek Allies); Darius III, Bessus, Mazaeus, Orontes II (Persians)

Outcome: Greco-Macedonian victory

Aftermath: The Persian defeat spelled the end for the Achaemenids and for Darius himself

Cannae

IT WAS HANNIBAL'S FINEST HOUR WHEN HE INFLICTED A CRUSHING DEFEAT ON THE ROMAN LEGIONS AT CANNAE DURING THE SECOND PUNIC WAR. UNFORTUNATELY FOR HIM, HE WAS UNABLE TO CAPITALIZE ON HIS GREAT VICTORY.

When the Second Punic War broke out in 218 BC, Rome and Carthage renewed their battle for Mediterranean dominance. This time, however, the Carthaginian strategy was different. Hannibal Barca, their greatest general, decided to make his way from Spain, where the fighting had started, through southern France and across the Alps into Italy to take the war to the enemy heartland. He would meet and beat the Romans on their own home ground. Having crossed the Alps – a feat the Romans considered impossible, especially since it took place in the depths of winter – Hannibal won two major victories over the Romans at Trebbia and Lake Trasimene, where he

The ruins of Carthage, the great Carthaginian city eventually destroyed by the Romans despite Hannibal's great victories at Tresimene and Cannae.

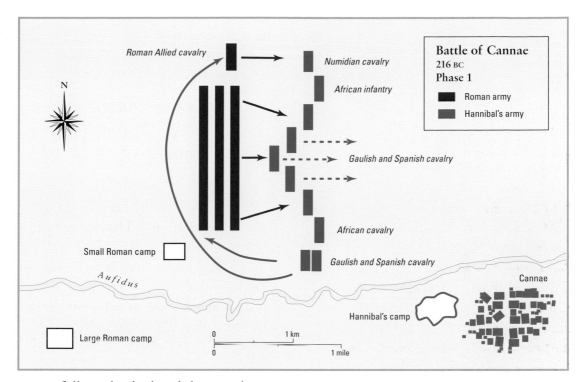

Phase 1 of the Battle of Cannae, illustrating the movements made by the Carthaginian and Roman armies.

successfully ambushed and destroyed an entire Roman army. The Roman response was to appoint Fabius Maximus dictator. His plan was to avoid further full-scale clashes with the invaders, and instead fight a war of attrition, relying on continual skirmishing to wear them down. However, these cautious tactics proved not to be popular with the Roman Senate, which was thirsting for a quick, decisive victory.

At the end of his term of office, Fabius Maximus was replaced by new Consuls: Gaius Terentius Varro, a blustering, bullying 'new man' who had used his wealth to climb the ladder to power, and

Lucius Aemilius Paullus, a quiet-spoken patrician. They were tasked with raising a new army to crush Hannibal once and for all. It was the largest single force the Roman Republic had put into the field.

FROM SKIRMISHES TO BATTLE

Having assembled a massive army of nearly 87,000 men, the two Consuls advanced on Cannae, an important Roman supply depot on the river Aufidus in south-eastern Italy, which the Carthaginians had

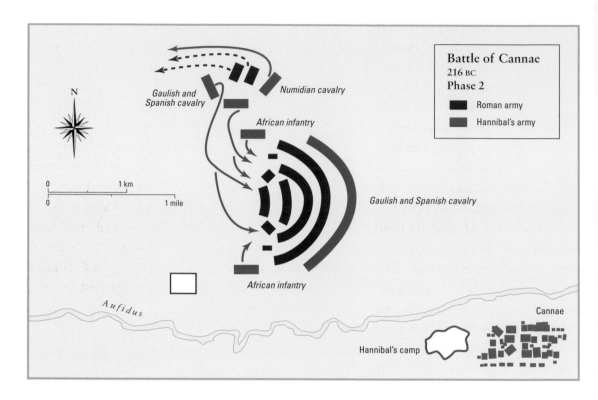

Battle of Cannae
216 BC
Phase 2

Roman army

Hannibal's army

N

0   1 km

0   1 mile

Gaulish and
Spanish cavalry

Numidian cavalry

African infantry

Gaulish and Spanish cavalry

African infantry

Aufidus

Cannae

Hannibal's camp

captured in the spring. On 31 July 216 BC, the advance guards of the two armies met along the banks of the river and started skirmishing. The battle proper began two days later. Roman military practice laid down that if two Consuls were present on the field, the command rotated between them, each holding it on alternate days.

Unfortunately for the Romans, rather than the more cautious Paullus, it was Varro, supremely confident that he would win an easy victory, who was in overall command when battle was joined. Varro's plan was brutally simple. Taking full

Phase 2 of the Battle of Cannae, illustrating the movements made by the Roman and Carthaginian armies.

advantage of their numerical superiority, his troops would grind their way forwards, smash through the Carthaginian battle line and then bludgeon Hannibal's men into defeat. Though Paullus, so it was later reported, was opposed to giving battle, he nevertheless fell in with Varro's wishes.

The Romans and Carthaginians took up their respective battle positions. Varro, following tradition, stationed his cavalry on the wings of his infantry, rank after rank of which was packed into the centre of the Roman battle line. Hannibal did the exact opposite, leaving light infantry to hold his centre and positioning his veteran heavy infantry with his cavalry on the flanks. As the Carthaginian line moved forwards, it began to bow into a crescent shape. This, too, was a break with convention, but the move had been carefully planned. The cavalry clashed first. Hasdrubal, Hannibal's brother in command of the Numidian contingent on the Carthaginian right, routed the Roman cavalry opposite him, driving much of it back across the river and scattering any stray infantry he found in his path. He then wheeled round behind the Roman centre to charge the cavalry on the other wing. It fled from the battlefield.

THE TRAP IS SPRUNG

It was Hannibal's turn to strike. He had taken up position with his light infantry in the centre of the Carthaginian line. He ordered it to fall back slowly, while the heavy infantry to the left and right held their positions. The Romans, scenting victory, were lured further and further forwards as the Carthaginians fell back. In fact, they were walking into a trap.

Hannibal ordered the infantry stationed on his wings to attack the enemy flanks. They closed in on the Romans like the jaws of a giant nutcracker. Simultaneously, the Carthaginian cavalry launched a massive assault on the Roman rear. The Romans were soon surrounded. They were packed so tightly together that many could not even raise their weapons, let alone fight.

It was an utter rout. Varro, who was blamed for the disaster, managed to escape; Paullus died alongside his men. Only 14,000 Romans managed to fight their way out of the encirclement and reach Canusium, the nearest town still in Roman hands. Between 3,500 and 4,500 Romans were taken prisoner. The rest perished on the battlefield.

FACT FILE

Cannae

Date: 2 August 216 BC

Location: Cannae, Italy

Historical Context: The Second Punic War (218–201 BC)

States Involved: Carthaginian Republic; Roman Republic

Commanders and Leaders: Hannibal and Hasdrubal Barca, Maharbal, Mago (Carthaginian Republic); Gaius Terentius Varro, Lucius Aemilius Paullus (Rome)

Outcome: Decisive Carthaginian victory

Actium

WHEN OCTAVIAN AND MARK ANTONY CLASHED AT SEA IN 31 BC, OCTAVIAN'S VICTORY SECURED HIM MASTERY OF THE ROMAN WORLD. TAKING THE NAME OF AUGUSTUS TO MARK THE EVENT, OCTAVIAN BECAME ROME'S FIRST EMPEROR.

Formal war between Octavian and Mark Antony started the year before Actium was fought. These two most influential of the three triumvirs had divided the Roman world between them after the assassination of Julius Caesar and the suppression of Brutus' revolt. There had been bad blood between them for years before this.

The agreement between the triumvirs had been that Octavian, Caesar's great-nephew and heir, should rule Rome and the west, while Antony became the overlord of Egypt and the east. Lepidus, the third triumvir, whose services were soon dispensed with, was left with the province of Africa. The division seemed straightforward but, as time went by, the relationship between Octavian and Antony became more and more strained. In an attempt to heal the rift, Octavia, Octavian's sister, was married to Antony in 40 BC, but three years later he left her and went back to Cleopatra, the Queen of Egypt and his former mistress.

The Romans could not forgive Antony for his apparent desertion. They had always detested Cleopatra and now were only too ready to believe that the infatuated Antony was preparing to install her as mistress of Rome by force. Capitalizing on the rising tide of public discontent, Octavian met with little or no opposition when he declared war. The stage was set for a final confrontation between the two great titans of the Roman world.

The Romans could not forgive Antony for his apparent desertion. They had always detested Cleopatra ...believing Antony was preparing to install her as mistress of Rome...

When war broke out, Antony was in Greece, accompanied by Cleopatra. There, he set up his headquarters at Patrae and established an advance base at Actium,

The map shows the movements made by the two fleets during the Battle of Actium, which culminated in Antony's retreat.

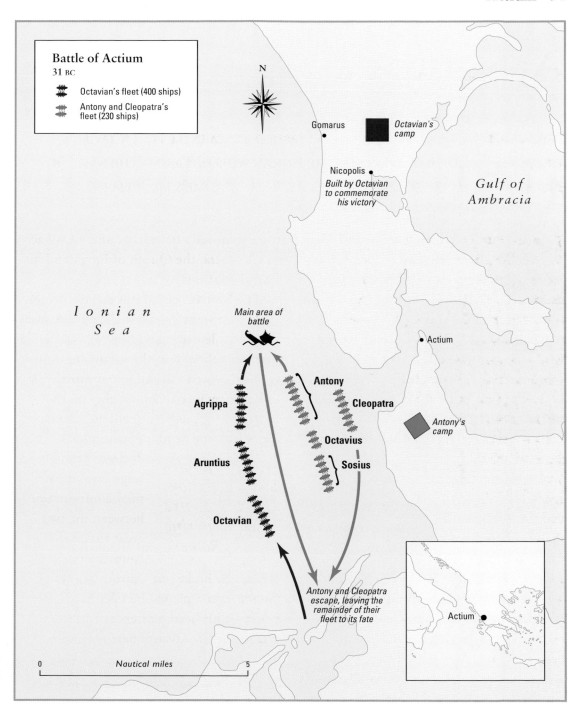

Battle of Actium
31 BC

Octavian's fleet (400 ships)

Antony and Cleopatra's
fleet (230 ships)

N

Gomarus

Octavian's
camp

Nicopolis
*Built by Octavian
to commemorate
his victory*

*Gulf of
Ambracia*

*I o n i a n
S e a*

*Main area of
battle*

Actium

Antony

Agrippa

Cleopatra

*Antony's
camp*

Octavius

Aruntius

Sosius

Octavian

*Antony and Cleopatra
escape, leaving the
remainder of their
fleet to its fate*

Actium

0   *Nautical miles*   5

near the mouth of the Ambracian Gulf on the coast of Epirus. The fear in Rome was that he was preparing to strike against Italy, but he realized that such a move

Believed to be the only relief carving of Cleopatra and her son Caesarion by Julius Caesar, at Dendara Temple in Egypt.

would be politically inopportune. Instead, he decided to play a waiting game, his aim being to force Octavian to cross the Adriatic to confront him.

It was probably Antony's intention to force Octavian to fight on land; he had a massive army, consisting of around 100,000 foot soldiers and 12,000 cavalry, under his command. However, the confrontation he was hoping for came about sooner than he had planned. Soon after midsummer, Octavian, with 400 ships, 80,000 infantry and 12,000 cavalry, crossed the Adriatic and set up a fortified camp of his own, some 16 km (10 miles) north of Antony's position at Actium.

Two months of manoeuvring and skirmishing followed, during which time Antony's position slowly but surely deteriorated. Octavian showed no inclination to confront him in full-scale battle; Antony, for his part, found it impossible to dislodge the Romans from the entrenched positions they had taken up around his camp. The real action was at sea, where Marcus Vipsanius Agrippa won control of the Ionian Islands, so cutting off Antony and Cleopatra from their supply bases in the Peloponnese.

By now, too, Antony's troops were becoming discontented, frustrated by the endless waiting, while sickness was also spreading in their ranks. Antony had two choices open to him: to escape by land through Macedonia, or to attempt to break through Agrippa's naval blockade and get back to Egypt by sea. Urged on by Cleopatra, who was desperate to return to her homeland the quickest possible way, he ordered his fleet to give battle.

ACTION AT ACTIUM

Antony drew his fleet up in front of the narrow strait leading to the Ambracian Gulf. He himself commanded the right wing, facing Agrippa. Before battle was finally joined on 2 September, he visited the captains of each vessel under his command to give his final instructions. He told them that they should remain inshore and fight a defensive battle. The idea was to let the Romans come to them. Cleopatra was tucked safely behind the main battle lines. Despite what Antony had said, Gaius Sosius and Marcus Octavius, who were in command of his left and centre, disregarded their orders. They allowed their galleys to be lured seawards by the enemy. The move gave the Roman ships the chance to exploit their manoeuvrability. They circled Antony's labouring galleys, attacking them with fire darts and other incendiary devices and dodging out of the way whenever their enemies tried to ram and board them.

What turned the tide of battle in the Romans' favour was the sudden flight of Cleopatra and her ships towards the Peloponnese. Antony abandoned his command and followed her. The fleet he had deserted battled on until late in the afternoon before surrendering to Agrippa. His army, at first unwilling to believe that Antony had fled, did not capitulate for another seven days. When it did, Octavian's victory was complete.

FACT FILE

Actium

Date: 31 BC

Location: Actium, Greece

States Involved: Rome; Egypt

Commanders and Leaders: Gaius Sosius, Marcus Octavius (Antony and his allies); Marcus Vipsanius Agrippa (Octavian and his allies)

Outcome: Decisive victory for Octavian

Aftermath: Octavian's victory secured him mastery of the Roman world, and he became Rome's first emperor

Teutoburg Forest

THE GERMAN WARRIOR-PRINCE ARMINIUS CHANGED THE COURSE OF HISTORY IN AD 9, WHEN HE WON A CRUSHING VICTORY OVER THREE ROMAN LEGIONS. IT WAS THE GREATEST SINGLE DEFEAT EVER INFLICTED ON ROME BY A BARBARIAN LEADER.

Sometimes, one man can alter the course of human history. Arminius, otherwise known as Hermann – the German name coined for him by Martin Luther centuries later – was just such an individual. Originally a prince from the Cherusci tribe, he had been taken to Rome as a hostage as a young boy. There, he was educated in Roman ways, eventually ending up being granted Roman citizenship and commissioned into the Roman army. Yet, as later events were to demonstrate, he never forgot his Germanic roots. Though on the surface he appeared to be totally Romanized, underneath he remained German to the core.

THE ROMANS IN GERMANY

Roman involvement in Germany began in the days of Julius Caesar, who carried out two short, sharp raids against the hostile German tribes immediately across the Rhine. After that, the Romans left Germany alone until 38 BC, when, according to the historian Cassius Dio, Marcus Agrippa became 'the second Roman to cross the Rhine ready for war'.

It was the emperor Augustus who decided to launch a war of out-and-out conquest with the main aim of incorporating the whole of Germany into his ever-expanding empire. He put Nero Claudius Drusus, his young stepson, in charge of the campaign. Drusus pushed eastwards as far as the river Elbe before dying of complications ensuing from a fall from his horse. Tiberius, his brother, succeeded him as commander-in-chief in Germany. Tiberius proved to be just as successful as his predecessor. In AD 5, he advanced even further east than Drusus

> *Roman involvement in Germany began in the days of Julius Caesar, who carried out two short raids against the hostile German tribes immediately across the Rhine.*

had managed when he led his legions across the river Elbe.

It seemed to Augustus – as it did to most Romans – that most of Germany had been pacified successfully. After Tiberius had been summoned away to deal with a revolt elsewhere, the emperor appointed Publius Quinctilius Varus to replace him. His orders to the new commander-in-chief were clear. He was to push ahead with the Romanization of the putative province.

The movements made by the Roman army and the Germanic tribes during the Battle of Teutoburg Forest.

VARUS BLUNDERS

All might have turned out well if Varus had not made a fatal mistake. Despite secret warnings that Arminius was not to be trusted, he put complete faith in the Cheruscan leader. Arminius, however, was secretly plotting the Romans' downfall and, by autumn AD 9, he was ready to strike. Arminius knew that Varus was about to withdraw from his summer camp at Minden on the river Weser and lead his legions back to their winter quarters. His plan was to get one of the German tribes to rise in revolt. Varus would surely move

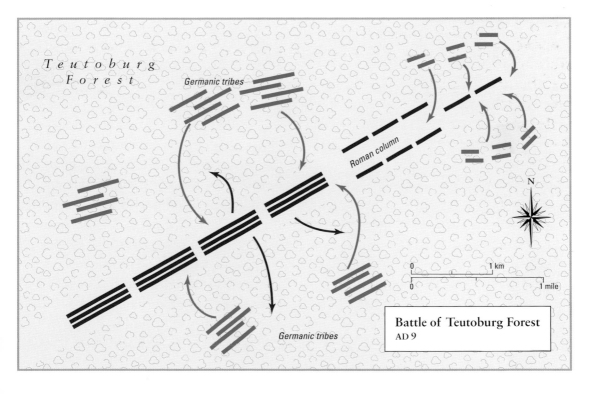

Germanic tribes

Teutoburg Forest

Roman column

N

Germanic tribes

0   1 km
0   1 mile

Battle of Teutoburg Forest
AD 9

A bust of the emperor Augustus, who sent his young stepson Nero Claudius Drusus off to conquer the German territories.

had anticipated, heading northwest with Arminius and his Cheruscan auxiliaries in the vanguard. Towards the end of the first day's march, Arminius persuaded Varus to let him and his men go off on their own to scout. The unsuspecting Varus agreed to the suggestion. In the meantime, he set up camp for the night.

ARMINIUS STRIKES

When the Romans resumed their march, things started to go wrong. The terrain became more and more difficult; then the weather broke. Lashed by gale-force winds and driving rain, the march slowed to a crawl.

This was Arminius' moment. As the day drew to its close, he launched a lightning attack. The onslaught took the Romans by surprise. Having inflicted heavy casualties, Arminius and his men melted into the twilight. Varus called his commanders together to decide what to do next. Retreat was not an option – the trail behind them had been blocked. He decided to burn his cumbersome baggage train and make a dash for the nearest river. There, his legions could make a stand while waiting for ferries to arrive to ship them to safety. It was not a bad plan, but once the legions had entered the Kalkriese Berg pass, they were doomed. Arminius unleashed the full weight of his forces for the first time. The

to put the rebellion down. Arminius and his allies would then be able to ambush the Romans en route, while they were still in what they thought of as friendly territory and so would be off their guard.

The plan worked to perfection. Varus and his troops did exactly what Arminius pass was so narrow that the legionaries could not deploy. All they could do was to struggle forwards as best they could in the face of the unrelenting German pressure. It was clear that the battle was nearly over. Varus, who already had been wounded, committed suicide rather than surrender. Many of his men followed their commander's example. Those who did not met a grisly fate. Arminius ordered them to be sacrificed to Donar, the German thunder-god.

FACT FILE

Teutoburg Forest

Date: AD 9

Location: Teutoburg Forest, Germany

States Involved: Germanic tribes, the Roman Empire

Commanders and Leaders: Arminius (Germanic Tribes); Publius Quinctilius Varus (Rome)

Outcome: Decisive Germanic victory

Aftermath: The greatest defeat ever inflicted on Rome by a barbarian leader; changed the course of history

Middle Ages

In the Middle Ages in feudal Europe, heavily armoured knights – mainly mounted, but sometimes fighting on foot – archers and foot soldiers were the mainstays of the typical medieval army.

Tours

WHEN THE MUSLIMS PUSHED NORTH FROM SPAIN INTO SOUTHERN FRANCE, IT SEEMED AS IF NOTHING COULD STAND IN THEIR WAY. THEN, AT TOURS, THEY SUFFERED A DECISIVE DEFEAT THAT SAVED WESTERN EUROPE FOR CHRISTIANITY.

Muslim expansion was the greatest threat to the Christian rulers of early medieval Europe. It began in the early 700s, when, after conquering the Iberian Peninsula, Umayyad forces pushed north across the Pyrenees into the heartlands of southern France. Led by Al-Samh ibn Malik, they overran the region stretching along the Mediterranean coast from the Pyrenees to the Rhone Valley, setting up their capital at Narbonne. They met little Christian resistance until 721, when Duke Odo of Aquitaine defeated them by lifting the siege of Toulouse and forcing them out of his realm.

Odo's success was short-lived. A decade later the Umayyads returned. Now led by Abd er Rahman, the Emir of Al-Andalus (modern-day Andalusia), they crushed Odo's forces at the battle of the river Garonne. Odo fled north to seek the help of the Franks.

ENTER CHARLES MARTEL

Charles Martel, mayor of the palace of Austrasia – one of the two kingdoms into

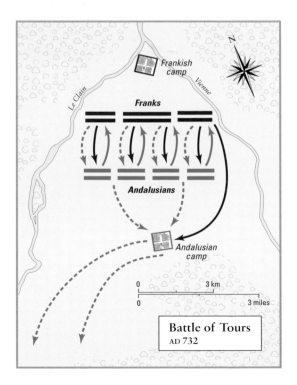

Battle of Tours
AD 732

The movements made by the Franks and the Andalusians during the Battle of Tours.

which Merovingian Gaul was now divided – was the man to whom the luckless Odo turned for help. The illegitimate son of Pepin of Heristal and a Frankish noblewoman called Alpaide, Charles had become mayor on the death of his father and, like him, was king in all but name. He promised to come to Odo's aid, provided that he would swear to submit to Frankish suzerainty. Odo had no choice but to yield to the demand. Charles then began to raise an army to take on the Muslim invaders.

Advancing south to intercept Abd er Rahman, Charles chose his battleground carefully. The army he had raised largely consisted of veteran Frankish infantry and may have been anywhere between 15,000 and 75,000 strong. Either way, the Franks were heavily outnumbered by the Muslim army, which was made up of light and heavy cavalry. The battleground Charles selected was a wooded plain at Moussais, situated around halfway between Poitiers and Tours. Having taken and burnt Poitiers to the ground, the Muslims were now advancing on the latter town. According to some contemporary sources, their goal was the Abbey of Saint Martin, where a fabulous treasure was reputed to be stored.

Charles Martel's soldiers were believed to have been attired and equipped like the combatant in this early engraving.

THE FRANKS STAND FIRM

The plain was undulating rather than level. This suited Charles, since it would force the Umayyad cavalry to charge uphill, putting them at a substantial disadvantage

from the start. What is clear is that the Frankish presence on the plain took Abd er Rahman completely by surprise. A week went by while he considered what best to do. The delay was to Charles' advantage, since it gave him the chance to summon reinforcements.

On 10 October 732, Abd er Rahman finally decided to give battle. He ordered his Berber and Arab cavalry to charge the Franks, expecting them to sweep through their opponents as they had done so often before. This time, it was to be a different story. As the Muslims attacked, the Franks promptly formed up into a large phalanx-like square to fight off attack after attack.

An Arab chronicler noted how 'the men of the North seemed like a sea that cannot be moved. Firmly they stood one close to another, forming, as it were, a bulwark of ice and with great blows of their swords they hewed down their foes'.

Finally, some Umayyads managed to break through and charge straight for Charles Martel who was saved by the intervention of his personal bodyguards. Then he played his trump card. He sent skirmishers to raid the Umayyad camp. Believing that they were about to be robbed of their booty, the Umayyad cavalry wavered and raced back to safeguard their loot. Their leader Abd er Rahman was cut down by the Franks while attempting to stop the retreat.

Expecting the Umayyad commanders to rally their forces and launch further

> *His success in the battle of Tours won Charles the cognomen of Martel (meaning the hammer) because of the merciless way he had hammered his foes into defeat.*

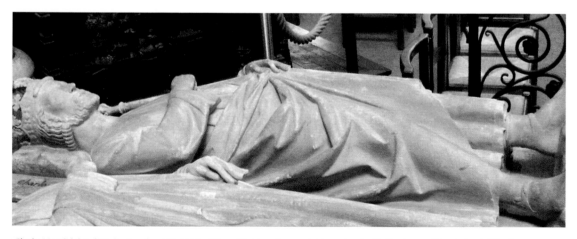

Charles Martel defeated Muslim invaders at the Battle of Tours. His triumphs put a decisive end to the Muslim threat to Merovingian-held lands.

attacks the following day, Charles ordered the Franks to reform their square. The attacks never came. That night, the surviving Umayyad generals started to quarrel amongst themselves and the only thing they could agree on was the need to continue their retreat. They did not stop until they had reached the safety of their stronghold in Spain.

His success in the battle of Tours won Charles the cognomen of Martel – meaning 'the hammer' – because of the merciless way he had hammered his foes into defeat. The victory did not mark the end of his campaigning, however, since the Umayyads still held the French territories they had conquered. In 736 and 739, Charles defeated them at Avignon, Nimes and outside Arles and Narbonne itself. Though the latter managed to hold out, Martel's triumphs put an end to the Muslim threat to Merovingian-held lands once and for all.

FACT FILE

Tours

Date: 10 October 732

Location: A plain at Moussais between Poitiers and Tours

States Involved: Merovingian Franks; Umayyad Caliphate

Commanders and Leaders: Charles Martel (Merovingian Franks); Abd er Rahman (Umayyad Caliphate)

Outcome: Decisive Frankish victory

Aftermath: Charles's victory put an end to the Muslim threat to Western Europe

Hastings

THE TURNING POINT IN THIS CRUCIAL BATTLE CAME WHEN A FEIGNED NORMAN RETREAT LURED THE SAXONS OUT OF THEIR RIDGE-TOP POSITION. WILLIAM THE CONQUEROR'S VICTORY ENSURED THAT HE, NOT HAROLD, RULED ENGLAND.

Hastings was not the only battle to be fought in England in 1066, but it was unquestionably the most significant. It was the deciding moment in the bitter contest between William the Conqueror and Harold Godwineson, the Earl of Wessex, as to who was the rightful heir to the childless Edward the Confessor and so would succeed to the English throne.

William's claim to the throne came about as a result of his marriage to Matilda, the daughter of Count Baldwin of Flanders and a direct descendant of Alfred the Great. More to the point, he also swore that Edward had actually promised him the succession as far back as 1051. When the old king finally died in January 1066, however, it was Harold, Edward's brother-in-law and the most powerful of the Saxon barons, who was proclaimed king in Edward's place. The outraged William immediately began planning an invasion. To some extent, his fury was justified, if the chroniclers of the time are to be believed. According to William, Harold had not only sworn allegiance to him after his shipwreck on the Norman coast two years previously, but had promised to support his efforts to secure the English crown. He was a perjurer – an oath-breaker who fully merited overthrow. The evidence was strong enough to convince Pope Alexander II to come out in William's support.

When the old king finally died...it was Harold, the most powerful of the Saxon barons, who was proclaimed king...William immediately began planning an invasion.

FACING TWO INVASIONS

Harold knew that a Norman attempt at invasion was a certainty, but this was by no means the only threat he had to face. The Vikings, too, were on the march. In

September, King Harald Hardrada, the ruler of Norway, landed an army in the estuary of the river Humber in the north-east of England to support Tostig, Harold's brother, who was also laying claim to the throne. Harold had to hurry north to deal with this Viking threat and his brother's bid for the crown.

The speed of Harold's march north took Harald Hardrada and Tostig, who had already defeated the northern Saxon earls,

Battle Abbey was built on the orders of Pope Alexander II by William the Conqueror as penance for killing so many Saxons in the Battle of Hastings. It is also reputed to be the site where Harold was wounded and killed.

totally by surprise. When the two armies clashed at Stamford Bridge in Yorkshire on 25 September, Harold defeated the invaders. He then force-marched his troops south to confront William, who had landed on the Sussex coast at or near Pevensey Bay on 28 September. Some historians believe this frantic march left

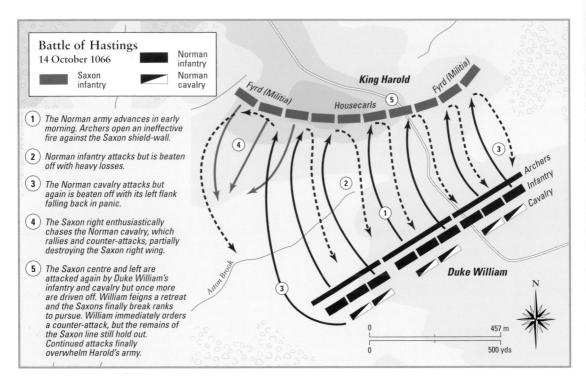

Battle of Hastings
14 October 1066

Norman infantry
Saxon infantry
Norman cavalry

King Harold

Fyrd (Militia)   Housecarls   Fyrd (Militia)

Duke William

Archers
Infantry
Cavalry

Aston Brook

1 The Norman army advances in early morning. Archers open an ineffective fire against the Saxon shield-wall.

2 Norman infantry attacks but is beaten off with heavy losses.

3 The Norman cavalry attacks but again is beaten off with its left flank falling back in panic.

4 The Saxon right enthusiastically chases the Norman cavalry, which rallies and counter-attacks, partially destroying the Saxon right wing.

5 The Saxon centre and left are attacked again by Duke William's infantry and cavalry but once more are driven off. William feigns a retreat and the Saxons finally break ranks to pursue. William immediately orders a counter-attack, but the remains of the Saxon line still hold out. Continued attacks finally overwhelm Harold's army.

0   457 m
0   500 yds

N

Harold's army exhausted and unfit to meet William's challenge. However, Harold pushed his men on and arrived just under 14 days later.

Saxon vs Normans

He reached the south coast, where William, who had erected a temporary wooden fort at Hastings, was sending out raiding parties to scout out the lay of the land. On the evening of 13 October, they told him of Harold's imminent approach.

The battle was fought the next day at Senlac Hill, 10 km (six miles) inland from Hastings. This time it was Harold who was

The movements made by the Saxon and Norman armies in the Battle of Hastings, resulting in victory for William.

taken by surprise by the sudden Norman attack. His troops hurriedly formed a shield wall along the crest of the ridge at the top of the hill. Harold took up a position on the highest point of the ridge with his housecarls (household warriors) around him. Below him were the Saxon levies that had rallied to his cause.

Below in the valley, William formed up his army in three ranks – archers to the fore, followed by heavy infantry and then, to the rear, the Norman knights. At around 9.00 am, the archers and infantry advanced to the attack. They were thrown back with heavy losses. When the knights advanced, they too failed to make any headway. The Bretons on the left began to fall back as a rumour that William had been killed spread. When some of the Saxons charged down the hill in pursuit, it looked as though Harold was on the brink of winning a great victory. William quickly intervened to rally the Bretons and so halt the potential retreat. His knights speedily cut down the foolhardy Saxons before they could retire. Now, William played his trump card. He ordered his knights to fall back in feigned retreat to tempt more Saxons down from the ridge.

The ruse succeeded. When the Norman knights and infantry attacked again, the Saxon shield wall began to buckle and then finally break. Bitter and bloody hand-to-hand fighting followed.

As twilight fell, Harold was wounded in the face by an arrow and then hacked to death by a group of Norman knights while trying to rally his troops. The Saxons were left leaderless – Gyrth and Leowine, Harold's other brothers, had already fallen earlier in the battle. Though some Saxons fought on to the end, the bulk of the Harold's army simply melted away into the Sussex Weald.

William's victory was complete. His sole surviving rival for the English throne was now dead. On Christmas Day 1066, he was crowned king in Westminster Abbey, and the course of English history was changed forever.

FACT FILE

Battle of Hastings

Date: 14 October 1066

Location: Hastings, England

States Involved: Normans; Saxons

Commanders and Leaders: William of Normandy, Odo of Bayeux (Normans); Harold Godwineson (Saxon)

Outcome: Decisive Norman victory

Aftermath: William's victory ensured that he would rule England. He was crowned king on Christmas Day in 1066

Arsuf

WHEN RICHARD I OF ENGLAND AND THE MUSLIM LEADER SALADIN CLASHED AT ARSUF DURING THE THIRD CRUSADE, IT WAS THE FIRST TIME THE TWO HAD MET IN BATTLE. SALADIN'S DEFEAT PUT AN END TO HIS REPUTATION FOR INVINCIBILITY.

Having successfully besieged Acre, which fell to the Crusaders in July 1191, the next logical step for Richard the Lionheart and his army was to move south to capture the port of Jaffa before turning inland to attack Jerusalem. The march was carefully planned. Richard deployed his forces in three divisions, each consisting of three columns. They kept to the coast as they marched, so that the Crusader fleet, which Richard relied on for supplies, could support them.

Richard's knights were stationed in the centre of each column, the baggage train to their left. To their right, the foot soldiers formed a defensive screen to protect them and their horses from attack by Saladin's skirmishing archers. Because this was such an exhausting task – Muslim observers commented admiringly on the way Richard's men kept plodding forwards,

The Crusaders were confronted by a huge Saracen army, 'arrayed as thick as drops of rain'...which was determined to contest their further advance...

their tunics bristling with arrow bolts until they looked like porcupines – Richard split his infantry in two, half of it marching along the seashore and half covering the Crusaders' landward flank, swapping the two halves around alternately.

Progress was slow – probably slower than Richard would have liked. It took the Crusaders two-and-a-half weeks to reach Jaffa, shadowed all the way by Saladin and his Saracen army. The Muslim leader's plan was simple. It was to launch a series of harassing raids on the landward flank and rear of the advancing Crusader columns. The first of these took place when Richard's troops were only a few kilometres out of Acre. Saladin's cavalry swooped down to attack the Crusader baggage train from the rear, but Richard and his knights, galloping from the vanguard, forced the attackers to withdraw. Saladin's aim was to force the break-up of the Crusader formation. If he could accomplish this, his cavalry could then sweep forwards for the kill.

A CHANGE OF TACTICS

On 7 September, as the Crusaders neared Arsuf, Saladin changed his tactics. Harassing Richard's army had brought him little success. Now he would give battle at a place of his own choosing. The Crusaders were confronted by a huge Saracen army – arrayed 'as thick as drops of rain', wrote one chronicler – which was determined to contest their further advance.

With the Saracens already drawn up in full battle array on his left flank, Richard arranged his dispositions carefully. He stationed his most experienced fighting

The diagram to the right shows the movements made by Richard the Lionheart and by Saladin during the Battle of Arsuf.

men – the Knights Templar and the Knights Hospitaller – in the van and rear of his formation, while the English and Norman knights were stationed in a central reserve around the king's dragon standard. The Crusaders were to remain on the

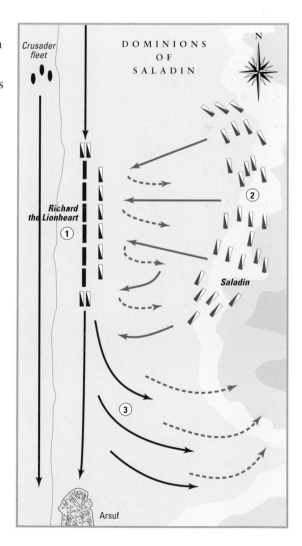

Battle of Arsuf
7 September 1191

- ▬ Crusader infantry
- ◣ Crusader cavalry
- ◣ Arab cavalry
- ← Crusader advance and attack
- ← Arab attack
- ◄--- Arab retreat

(1) The Crusaders, led by Richard the Lionheart, head for the port of Jaffa, via Arsuf, which is required to supply the Jerusalem campaign.

(2) On the march south, they are constantly attacked by Saladin's cavalry riding down from the hills.

(3) As they reach Arsuf, Richard orders his cavalry to attack Saladin's cavalry, forcing them to flee.

An ancient citadel, which served as a fortress for the Crusaders, the Tower of David is near the Jaffa Gate entrance to the old city of Jerusalem.

defensive until Richard judged that the time was right. His intention was to leave the fighting to his infantry, holding his knights back until the Saracens exhausted themselves. If the knights charged too soon, they would run the risk of becoming scattered and vulnerable to counter-attack from the Saracens.

For most of the long, hot day – the battle started at around 9.00 am – the Crusaders stubbornly stood their ground and repelled attack after attack. Trumpets sounding, war drums beating and cymbals clashing, Saladin's cavalry repeatedly charged, wheeled round and charged again, each time pressing closer and closer in on the Crusader ranks. They were supported by Arab pikemen and Nubian archers, who, as one chronicler put it, 'filled the air so full of arrows, they dimmed the sunlight'. Richard's crossbowmen returned the Nubian fire. For their part, the knights waited more and more impatiently for the six-trumpet call that was the agreed signal for them to charge the enemy.

THE CRUSADERS CHARGE

The warrior-monk Brother Garnier de Nablus, the commander of the Knights Hospitaller, was growing particularly concerned about the losses to his knights' horses. He appealed to Richard to let him attack, but the king told him to continue to be patient. Eventually, he could stand the waiting no longer. He and his knights independently charged their Saracen tormentors. Luckily for him, the Nubians, convinced that the Crusaders would never break formation, had just dismounted in order to improve their aim and speed up their rate of fire. The Hospitallers swiftly overran them and then began driving back the Saracen right.

Richard, although angered by the Hospitallers' disobedience, reacted quickly, signalling a general advance. The Knights

Templar, supported by the Breton and Angevin knights, charged the Saracen left, while he led the knights he had kept back in reserve in an attack on Saladin's centre. As the whole Crusader line surged forwards, the Saracens were taken by surprise. They fell back and then fled the field, while the Crusaders captured and looted their camp. Richard had scored an impressive victory.

FACT FILE
Arsuf

Date: 7 September 1191

Location: Arsuf, Israel

Historical Context: The Third Crusade (1189–1192)

States Involved: English Crusaders; Muslim Ayyubids

Commanders and Leaders: Richard I, Robert de Sablé, Garnier de Nablus (Crusaders); Saladin, Gokbori, Al-Adil I, Kaimaz an-Nejimi, Ala ad-Din, Musek the Kurd, Kaimaz al-Adili, Lighush, Alim ad-Din Kaisar. Akhar Aslem, Saif ad-Din Yazkoj, Al-Gheidi, Jawali, Aiyaz al-Mehran (Ayyubids)

Outcome: Decisive English victory

Aftermath: Saladin's defeat put an end to his reputation for invincibility

Bannockburn

ALTHOUGH THE ENGLISH DID NOT FORMALLY RECOGNIZE SCOTTISH INDEPENDENCE FOR ANOTHER 14 YEARS, ROBERT BRUCE'S DEFEAT OF EDWARD II AT BANNOCKBURN IN 1314 WAS THE DECISIVE VICTORY OF A LONG, DRAWN-OUT WAR.

By 1314, after 18 years of war, all Scotland north of the Firth of Forth was finally free from English domination. That spring, Edward Bruce, King Robert's brother, laid siege to Stirling Castle, one of only two strongpoints in the country still in English hands. Having failed to bring about its speedy fall, he and Sir Philip de Mowbray, the garrison's commander, agreed that if English reinforcements had not managed to raise the siege by Midsummer's Day, de Mowbray would surrender the castle to the Scots. Edward acted without consulting his brother, who was angered by the arrangement. The years of guerrilla warfare he had waged had worn down the English at relatively little cost to the Scots. Now, if Edward II came to de Mowbray's assistance, Robert faced having to fight a major battle. If he was beaten by

> *The Scottish forces took up position to the south of the castle, where the old Roman road from Falkirk ran through the New Park, a royal hunting ground.*

Edward, he might lose the crown he had struggled so hard to secure.

EDWARD MARCHES NORTH

Edward II was well aware that the loss of Stirling would deal a devastating blow to his already shaky prestige. His ambitious plan was not simply to raise the siege of the castle, but to go on to reconquer all the Scottish territory the English had lost since the death of his father. Early that summer, he marched north at the head of an army of around 20,000 men, reaching Berwick-upon-Tweed in mid-May.

Leaving Berwick in early June, Edward II advanced north via Edinburgh, reaching Falkirk, only 24 km (15 miles) short of his destination, on 23 June. Some seasoned veterans of previous Scottish campaigns –

The map on the right shows the movements made by the Scottish and English armies during the Battle of Bannockburn.

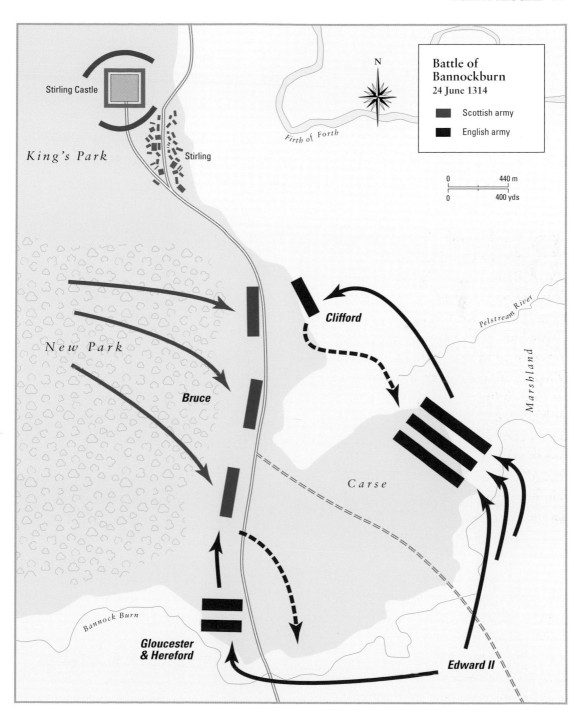

Battle of
Bannockburn
24 June 1314

Scottish army

English army

Stirling Castle

King's Park

Stirling

New Park

Bruce

Clifford

Carse

Marshland

Bannock Burn

Gloucester
& Hereford

Edward II

Firth of Forth

Pelstream River

notably the earls of Hereford, Gloucester and Pembroke – had accompanied him on his long march. Other powerful noblemen had refused to answer the royal call to arms. They had no confidence in Edward's military skills.

Robert, who had had months to prepare for Edward's coming, mustered between 6,000 and 7,000 spearmen, men-at-arms and archers, plus 500 cavalry and 2,000 so-called 'small folk', to oppose him. The spearmen, by far the greatest part of the Scottish army, were divided into three schiltrons, or divisions. Breaking with

Stirling Castle has been besieged at least eight times and several Scottish monarchs have been crowned there.

Scottish military tradition, the king had taught them how to fight on the move.

The Scottish forces took up position to the south of the castle, where the old Roman road from Falkirk ran through the New Park, a royal hunting ground. To the east, the Bannock and Pelstream burns and the marshlands around them were fine natural obstacles. In addition, Robert had his men dig 'pots' – small 1-metre (3-feet) deep concealed pits – along the roadway to deny its use to Edward's knights. His aim was to block Edward's advance and force him away from the road on to the Carse, the low-lying plain to the right. Once the English army was on the Carse, it would have to fight on a narrow front, negating its numerical superiority.

BATTLE IS JOINED

The battle began on 25 June, when Edward responded to de Mowbray's pleas for help – the garrison commander had made his way to the English camp – by ordering 500 knights to assist him. One of the Scottish schiltrons moved to intercept them. The knights charged repeatedly, but failed to break through the thrusting wall of spears confronting them. Then the Scots did something completely unexpected. They charged the cavalry. It was the last straw for the knights. Totally demoralized, they fell back to report their failure.

In the meantime skirmishing had been taking place elsewhere, in which Robert personally had become involved. As the English vanguard forded the Bannock Burn, Henry de Bohun, a young English knight, charged forwards to engage him in single combat. Robert swiftly killed him with a single blow of his battleaxe. For the Scots, it was an inspiring end to the day.

That night, Robert considered his options carefully. His first thought was to remain on the defensive, but reports of the enemy's lowered morale persuaded him to attack. At dawn the next day he took the offensive, marshalling his troops in four divisions and marching them towards the English lines. The Earl of Gloucester charged to meet them, but he was killed and the charge broken.

The Scots marched on remorselessly. Surrounded on three sides by the waters of the Bannock Burn and unable to deploy, the English were soon in a state of complete confusion. Many of them tried to flee across the burn. When the news broke that Edward had taken flight, the English resistance collapsed, and they fell back in rout. Edward II had lost between 4,000 and 11,000 men. Denied refuge in Stirling Castle by de Mowbray, he made for Dunbar and safety. He was never to return to Scotland again, and Robert the Bruce's position was greatly strengthened.

Agincourt

THE YOUNG HENRY V'S ATTACK ON FRANCE IN 1415 WAS INTENDED AS A SPOILING RAID RATHER THAN A WAR OF CONQUEST, BUT THIS DID NOT STOP HIM WINNING ONE OF THE GREATEST VICTORIES OF THE HUNDRED YEARS WAR.

When Henry V of England landed his army near Harfleur in northern France in August 1415, probably the last thing on his mind was the conquest of the entire kingdom. Indeed, during the protracted negotiations with the French that had taken up much of the previous year, he had indicated his willingness to give up his claim to the French throne in exchange for 1.6 million crowns and the formal recognition of the fact that he was the rightful ruler of the territories his predecessors had conquered.

Henry was prepared to go further. He was also willing to marry Catherine, the daughter of the half-mad Charles VI, if the French king agreed to pay Henry another 2 million crowns as a dowry. Charles baulked at the price. The negotiations broke down with war as the inevitable result.

He was willing to marry Catherine, the young daughter of the half-mad Charles VI, if the French king agreed to pay Henry another 2 million crowns as a dowry.

A DISASTROUS CAMPAIGN

Almost from the onset, Henry's campaign did not go according to plan. He had counted on taking Harfleur quickly, then advancing east to Paris and carrying on south to Bordeaux. In the event, the town did not fall until 22 September, by which time the campaigning season was coming to an end. Instead, Henry decided to launch an armed raid across Normandy to reach the English-held port of Calais, where his army could be re-embarked safely.

It is estimated that Henry had 900 men-at-arms (each with two retainers) and 5,000 longbowmen under command when he left Harfleur on 8 October. To speed up the march, the king left his artillery and baggage train behind. His men carried

The map shows the movements made by the French and the English during the Battle of Agincourt.

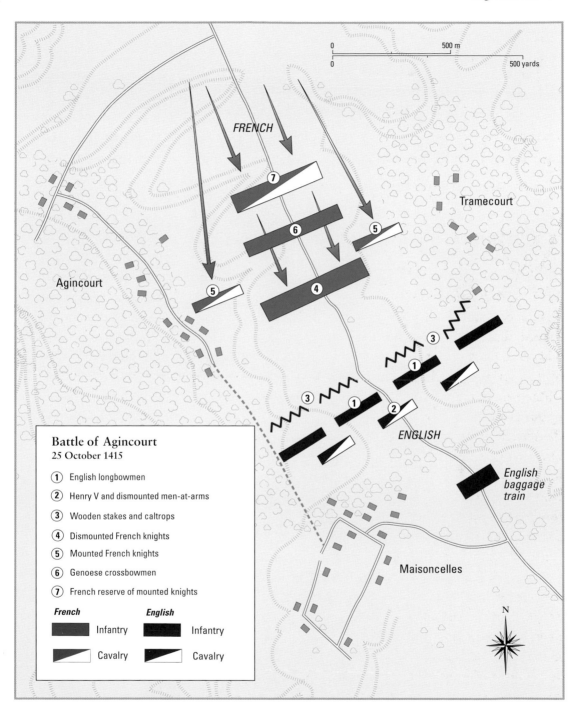

Battle of Agincourt
25 October 1415

1. English longbowmen
2. Henry V and dismounted men-at-arms
3. Wooden stakes and caltrops
4. Dismounted French knights
5. Mounted French knights
6. Genoese crossbowmen
7. French reserve of mounted knights

French

Infantry

Cavalry

English

Infantry

Cavalry

FRENCH

Tramecourt

Agincourt

ENGLISH

English
baggage
train

Maisoncelles

N

rations for only eight days – after that, they would have to live off the land.

Meanwhile, the French had not been idle. They were massing a 20,000-strong army. Under the command of the highly regarded Marshal Boucicaut, the French advance guard shadowed Henry every inch of the way, blocking him every time he attempted to cross the River Somme. Eventually, Henry got his men over the river some distance upstream of his originally intended crossing point. By now, the weather had turned foul, which only added to his problems. His men were soaked, starving and suffering from dysentery. Hurrying north again, he got to within 32 km (20 miles) of Calais before being brought to bay. Henry had no choice but to stand and fight for it. Fortunately for him, all was not well in the French camp, either. Boucicaut, Charles d'Albret, the Constable of France, and other nobles – all jealous of each other – were busy quarrelling about who should be in overall command and what battle tactics should be employed. By the time they finally formed up their army, Henry had seized the initiative. The weather also favoured him. An overnight downpour had turned the newly ploughed fields over which the French would have to advance into a quagmire.

The English had taken up a strong defensive position along the ridge that ran between the woods of Agincourt and Tramecourt, the men-at-arms holding the centre with the archers stationed on either flank, sheltering behind a forest of stakes they had driven into the ground to protect them against the French cavalry. Realizing that the French attack had been delayed

> *By the time they finally formed their army, Henry had seized the initiative. The weather also favoured him. An overnight downpour had turned the fields into a quagmire.*

An eighteenth-century engraving of Henry V of England (1386–1422), who was surprised by his victory at Agincourt and immortalized by Shakespeare.

– it took three hours to ready their three battle lines – Henry ordered his troops to move forward to take up a new position. The move ensured that the charging French would be within striking range of his longbows from the start.

At last, the French were ready. Their first line, consisting of 8,000 dismounted men-at-arms, slowly lumbered forwards towards Henry's positions. The undisciplined French cavalry forced a way through them and launched a disorganized charge. Henry's archers replied by unleashing a storm of arrows. The cavalry fell back onto the first line, throwing it into disorder. Nevertheless, the French continued to press forwards, forcing Henry's men-at-arms to give ground.

The fighting was hand-to-hand and extremely bitter. Having exhausted their supplies of arrows, even the archers joined in, attacking the French flanks. Eventually, the French fell back – only to collide with their second line, which was pushing forwards in support. As the battle raged, d'Albret and other French notables fell; some 1,500 of them, according to the chroniclers, were taken prisoner. Some were held for ransom, but others were killed on Henry's orders.

Why he sanctioned the slaughter is unclear, but he may have feared they might take up arms again and join a raiding party that was threatening his rear. Either way, the surviving French had no one left to rally them. Disconsolately, they fled the field. Against all the odds, Henry had won an amazing victory. Agincourt is now a byword for English bravery and strength in battle, immortalized in Shakespeare's lines in *Henry V*:

'We few, we happy few, we band of brothers;
For he today that sheds his blood with me
Shall be my brother.'

FACT FILE
Agincourt

Date: 25 October 1415

Location: Agincourt, France

Historical Context: The Hundred Years War (1337–1453)

States Involved: England; France

Commanders and Leaders: Henry V (England); Marshal Boucicaut, Charles d'Albret (France)

Outcome: Decisive English victory

Aftermath: Henry V's attack on France remains one of the greatest victories of the Hundred Years War; Shakespeare immortalized the victory in *Henry V*.

Siege of Orléans

THE EIGHT-MONTH SIEGE OF ORLÉANS BY THE ENGLISH COLLAPSED NINE DAYS AFTER JOAN OF ARC ARRIVED THERE IN MAY 1429. IT WAS HER FIRST GREAT MILITARY VICTORY AND A DECISIVE TURNING POINT OF THE HUNDRED YEARS WAR.

Determined to assert their military superiority, the English again began campaigning in France in 1428. They already held much of the northern part of the country. Now 6,000 troops, commanded by the Earl of Salisbury, headed south. Joined by the Duke of Bedford and 4,000 reinforcements from Normandy, the English captured Chartres and several other important towns by late August. They then moved forwards down the Loire Valley towards Orléans. Salisbury's plan was to isolate Orléans and then lay siege to the city.

THE SIEGE BEGINS

Salisbury's forces, now only some 4,000 strong since many of his troops were garrisoning the places he had captured, arrived south of Orléans on 12 October. They were confronted by the substantial fortifications the French had built on the south bank of the Loire – the city was on the northern side. The fortifications consisted of a barbican and a twin-towered gatehouse, called Les Tourelles. By 23 October, Salisbury's men had succeeded in ousting the French, who fell back into the city.

Things appeared to be going well for the English, but the next day calamity struck, when Salisbury was mortally wounded. The Earl of Suffolk, his replacement, was a far less aggressive commander and with winter coming on, he pulled back from the city and ordered his troops to take up winter quarters. Only Sir William Glasdale and a small force were left behind to garrison Les Tourelles. This was a strategic error.

> *Suffolk was a far less aggressive commander and with winter coming on, he pulled back from the city and ordered his troops to take up winter quarters.*

Joan of Arc is not only a martyr and a saint; she remains a folk heroine in France, immortalized in paintings, sculptures and friezes.

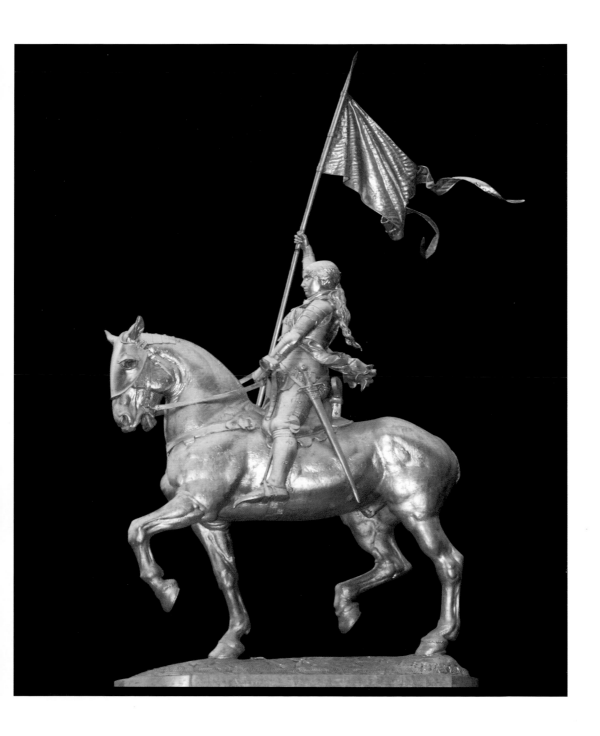

TIGHTENING THE SIEGE

Such was the situation in early December when the Earl of Shrewsbury arrived with reinforcements, took over command and ordered the English back to the city. Transferring the bulk of his troops to the Loire's northern bank, he began to build strong forts to the west, south and north-east of the city, with one on the Ile de Charlemagne in the river itself.

Shrewsbury's plan was to starve the French into submission. However, he lacked the manpower to surround the city completely. French reinforcements, led by Jean Dunois, who took charge of the city's defence, started to arrive. Even though 1,500 Burgundians reinforced Shrewsbury, he was soon heavily outnumbered. Moreover, further down the Loire at Blois, the French were assembling an army with which to raise the siege.

Shrewsbury was by no means dismayed. In February 1429, he defeated the French relieving force after the Count of Clermont, its commander, had injudiciously attacked an English supply column. He also knew the situation within Orléans was becoming desperate. Then he suffered a major setback. The citizens of Orléans asked the Duke of Burgundy to put them under his protection. Bedford, who was Henry VI's regent in France, refused to countenance the proposal. In retaliation, the Burgundians repudiated their alliance with the English and withdrew their men from the siege.

JOAN OF ARC ARRIVES

It was now that Joan of Arc came onto the scene. Appearing at the French Dauphin's court at Chinon that March, she convinced Charles that she had been inspired by the voices of the saints, who said God had chosen her to lead the French to victory. The following month, Charles let her take command of a supply column the French were planning to send to Orléans. Joan entered the city on 29 April. Dunois then left for Blois. On his return, he brought Charles' relieving force with him.

On 4 May, the French took the offensive, attacking the fort at St Loup to the east of the city. Shrewsbury tried to come to its aid, but failed in the attempt. Two days later, they struck again – this time at the other places the English had fortified so painstakingly. Shrewsbury responded by withdrawing all his troops from the south bank of the Loire, except for the garrison of Les Tourelles and the neighbouring barbican.

Fighting started around 8.00 am on 8 May with an assault on the barbican.

The map shows the positioning of English troops around the city during the Siege of Orléans.

When Joan was wounded, Dunois considered calling off the attack, but she returned to the battlefield and persuaded him to change his mind. Finally, inspired by her bravery, the French managed to break into the barbican. At the same time, they managed to set fire to the drawbridge linking the barbican with Les Tourelles, which simultaneously came under attack by a force of militia from within the city. By nightfall, all English resistance on the south bank had collapsed and the French were masters of the entire position. Shrewsbury played his last card. The next morning, he prepared to give battle on the north bank. Joan realized that this was a trap and counselled Dunois against attacking. Shrewsbury had no choice but to withdraw. The siege of Orléans was over. Joan of Arc's reputation was enhanced among the French, but, for the English, she became a figure of hate.

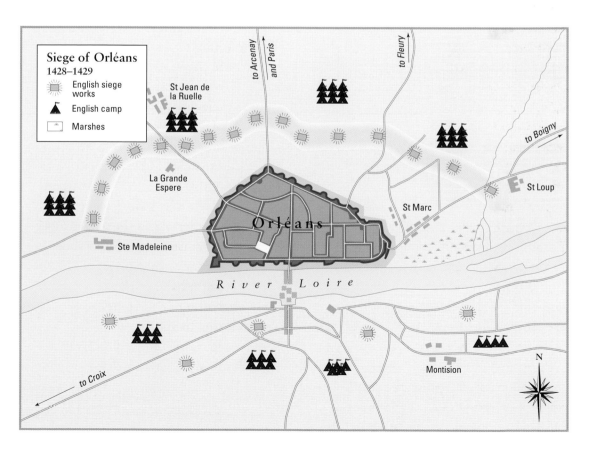

Siege of Orléans
1428–1429
- English siege works
- English camp
- Marshes

to Arcenay and Paris
to Fleury
to Boigny
St Jean de la Ruelle
La Grande Espere
Orléans
St Marc
St Loup
Ste Madeleine
River Loire
to Croix
Montision
N

Fall of Constantinople

WHEN THE BYZANTINE CAPITAL FELL TO THE OTTOMAN TURKS IN 1453, THE EVENT MARKED THE END OF 1,000 YEARS OF EMPIRE AND THE EMERGENCE OF A NEW AND POTENTIALLY DEADLY CHALLENGE TO CHRISTIANITY IN WESTERN EUROPE.

When the Ottoman Sultan Mehmet II rode in triumph into Constantinople on 28 May 1453, it was the end of a thousand years of the Byzantine Empire. After a siege lasting 53 days, its fortress-capital had fallen after a fierce, but ultimately futile, resistance. 'The blood flowed in the city like rainwater in the gutter after a sudden storm', a contemporary chronicler recorded. Constantine XI Palaeologus, the last Byzantine emperor, was among the dead, slain by an unknown Ottoman assailant in the ruins.

When the news of the city's fall reached Western Europe, it was greeted with consternation. Every earlier attempt to capture it had failed, so why had the Ottomans succeeded on this occasion? Was it simply because Mehmet had equipped his army with the latest in Western weaponry, including giant siege cannon to batter down the city's ancient fortifications? Or was there a cocktail of differing reasons? One thing was abundantly clear. In Mehmet, who had become sultan only two years previously, the defeated Byzantines had acquired a formidable adversary, who was young, ambitious and determined to conquer.

Recognizing the ever-growing Ottoman threat, Constantine sank his pride and appealed to Pope Nicholas V for help. None was forthcoming, though some Italian mercenaries, under the command of Giovanni Giustiniani, eventually did arrive in the city. Additionally, Constantine did his best to improve his capital's fixed defences. He

> *When news of the city's fall reached Western Europe, it was greeted with consternation. Every earlier attempt to capture it had failed; why had the Ottomans succeeded...?*

The map on the right shows the movements of the Ottoman forces that brought about the fall of Constantinople.

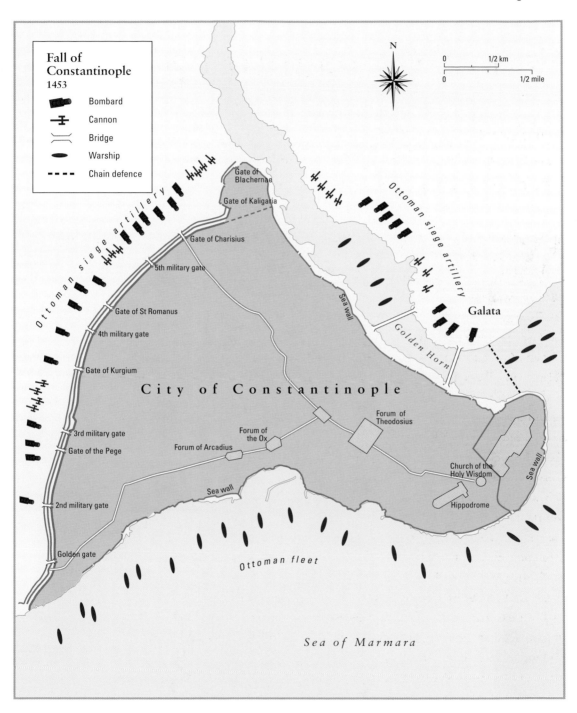

Fall of
Constantinople
1453

Bombard
Cannon
Bridge
Warship
Chain defence

N

0   1/2 km
0   1/2 mile

Ottoman siege artillery

Gate of
Blachernae

Gate of Kaligaria

Gate of Charisius

5th military gate

Ottoman siege artillery

Galata

Gate of St Romanus

Sea wall

4th military gate

Golden Horn

Gate of Kurgium

City of Constantinople

Forum of
Theodosius

3rd military gate

Forum of
the Ox

Gate of the Pege

Forum of Arcadius

Church of the
Holy Wisdom

2nd military gate

Sea wall

Hippodrome

Sea wall

Golden gate

Ottoman fleet

Sea of Marmara

had the massive Theodosian Walls repaired and the fortifications in the northern Blachernae district strengthened. He also ordered a massive boom to be stretched across the entrance to the Golden Horn to prevent any Ottoman troop transports from getting into the harbour from the Sea of Marmara.

BOMBARDING THE CITY

The Ottomans reached the city in full strength on 5 April 1453. Mehmet's army consisted of some 80,000 seasoned troops, including 12,000 elite Janissaries and many thousands of irregulars. Constantine and Giustiniani had only 5,000 Byzantines and 2,000 Italians to man the city's fortifications. Weight of numbers, however, was not necessarily the main problem confronting the Christians – Constantinople's defences had been a match for numerically superior forces before. This time, though, the Ottomans had brought many cannon with them. Some were so big and cumbersome that it

Mosaic of Virgin Mary, Jesus Christ and other saints in Hagia Sofia, the chief Byzantine church in Constantinople. For 500 years after the fall, it served as the principal mosque of Istanbul, as the city is now known.

took up to three hours to reload them once they had been fired, but they possessed awesome destructive power. The Ottoman artillerymen immediately started battering away at the Theodosian Walls, but, as fast as they opened up breaches in the walls, the defenders managed to repair them.

Both sides were more focused on the sea during the opening stages of the siege than they were on what was happening on land. Here, the Byzantines had the advantage; although outnumbered, their ships and sailors were superior to those of their foes. Two Ottoman attempts to break through the boom were repulsed. After the failure of the second naval attack, Mehmet ordered part of his fleet to be transported on rollers overland into the Golden Horn. Constantine ordered fire ships to attack the Ottomans, but the attempt failed. As a result, he was obliged to reinforce the Golden Horn walls at the expense of his landward defences.

On land, the siege was not going that well for the Ottomans. When their initial attacks on the Theodosian Walls were turned back by the Byzantine defenders, Mehmet turned to mining underneath them. The Byzantines promptly started countermining to neutralize the threat. The first Ottoman mine was detected on 18 May. The rest were located and destroyed a few days later.

THE FINAL BREAKTHROUGH

By now, the siege had been in progress for seven weeks. Many advised Mehmet to withdraw, but he decided to make a last all-out attempt to bring about the fall of the city.

Shortly before midnight on 28 May, Mehmet ordered his *bashi-bazouk* irregulars into action. After several hours of hard fighting, they were thrown back with heavy losses, but their attack succeeded in wearing down the defenders. Mehmet's Anatolian regiments then took up the attack. When they too failed, he threw in his Janissaries. Slowly but surely, they drove back the badly wounded Giustiniani and his Italians, who were manning the Blachernae defences.

Things started to go equally badly for Constantine, who was leading the Byzantines defending the walls in the Lycus Valley. Locating an unguarded sally port, the Ottomans poured through it and on into the city. Constantine was forced to fall back. He was killed leading a last desperate counter-attack against his Ottoman foes. With his death, Byzantine resistance collapsed.

Constantinople fell. Mehmet allowed his men to plunder the city for three days before restoring order. It was a devastating blow to Christianity as this Byzantine jewel slipped into Muslim control.

From Renaissance to Revolution

With the gunpowder revolution, the way in which battles were fought changed forever. Armies grew bigger. They were better led by commanders who made a special study of the art and science of war.

Lepanto

THE LAST GREAT BATTLE BETWEEN GALLEYS IN HISTORY, LEPANTO TRANSFORMED THE NAVAL BALANCE OF POWER IN THE MEDITERRANEAN IN FAVOUR OF CHRISTIANITY. DURING THE BATTLE, DON JOHN OF AUSTRIA ANNIHILATED THE OTTOMAN FLEET.

Paradoxically, Don John's success in the battle of Lepanto stemmed from an initial failure. The Christians could not muster a fleet in time to come to the aid of Venice and raise the siege of Famagusta in Cyprus, which had been their original intention. As a consequence, the city fell to the Ottoman Turks.

It was perhaps not surprising that it took time for Don John of Austria, who had been made commander of the fleet of the so-called Holy League, to gather the participating vessels together as ships from six Christian powers – Venice, Spain, the Papal States, Genoa, Savoy and Malta – were involved. At full strength, his fleet consisted of some 217 galleys and six huge Venetian-built galleasses. Opposing him, Ali Pasha – Selim II's grand admiral – had 230 galleys and 66 smaller vessels under

Despite Genoese opposition, voiced by their admiral ... Don John decided the best course of action was to offer immediate battle. Ali Pasha met with similar reservations...

his command. These two enormous fleets were to battle it out for supremacy over the Mediterranean region.

PREPARING FOR BATTLE

With battle still raging in Cyprus and Ottoman squadrons ravaging the Aegean and Ionian seas, Don John set sail from Sicily on 25 September 1571 for the Gulf of Corinth and Corfu, where he and his commanders held a council of war. Despite Genoese opposition, voiced by their admiral, Gian Andrea Doria, Don John decided the best course of action was to offer immediate battle. Ali Pasha met with similar reservations from some of his subordinates. Nevertheless, he, too,

The map shows the movements of the Christian and Ottoman fleets during the Battle of Lepanto.

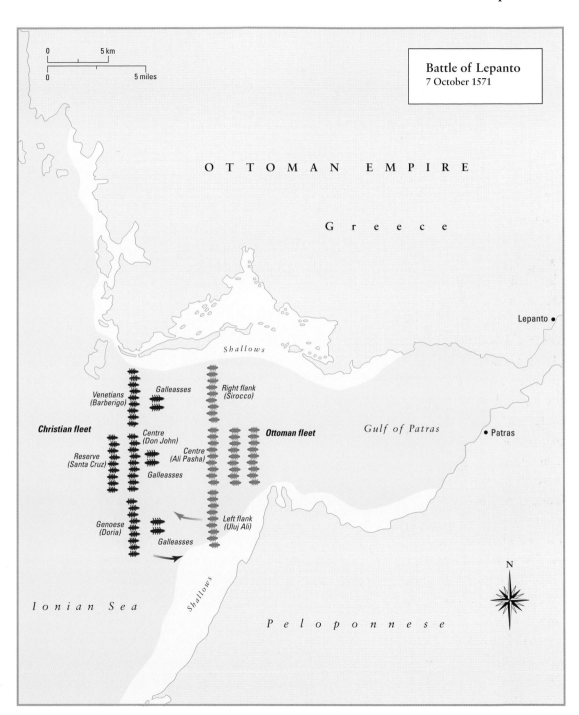

Battle of Lepanto
7 October 1571

decided to risk a clash. The Ottomans left their base at Lepanto and sailed west to intercept the Christian fleet.

The two fleets sighted each other in the Gulf of Patras on the morning of 7 October. Don John had already marshalled his ships in three divisions to form an 8-km (5-mile) battle line; the Venetians on the left, the Genoese on the right and himself in the centre. A reserve force brought up the rear. Each division was led by a pair of galleasses, each of which carried 50 heavy guns and some 500 arquebusiers.

Their firepower far outweighed that of the Ottoman vessels opposing them. Ali Pasha had also drawn up his fleet in three divisions, his battle line taking the shape of a crescent with a reserve behind the crescent. His left wing was stronger than his right one, indicating that his probable intention was to try to envelop the Christian right wing. He placed himself in the centre of the formation.

> *Don John was wounded and Ali Pasha killed. His head was cut off, impaled on a pike and raised high for all to see ... Ottoman morale collapsed and their centre fell apart.*

Fortification of ancient Famagusta, Cyprus, which fell to the Ottomans after a long siege in 1570–1571 and sparked the Lepanto response.

THE FLEETS ENGAGE

The battle started shortly after 10.00 am, with Don John's galleasses breaking through the Ottoman line. By midday, the action had degenerated into a mass of individual and group melees as the contending galleys closed in on one another to grapple and board. In the centre the *Real* and the *Sultana* – the flagships of the two commanders-in-chief – were battling it out. At their third attempt, Don John's men were able to board the *Sultana*. In the fierce fighting that ensued, Don John was wounded and Ali Pasha killed. His head was cut off, impaled on a pike and raised high for all around to see. At this point Ottoman morale collapsed and their centre fell apart as a result.

Things were going better for the Ottomans on their left wing, where Uluj Ali had taken advantage of a gap between the Genoese and the Christian centre. Uluj Ali was an Italian by birth who had started off as a pirate, converted to Islam and eventually become Pasha of Algiers. He slipped through the gap to strike at the Christian galleys. With the seven galleys under his command, he attacked three Maltese vessels – including the *Capitana*, the Maltese flagship – while the 16 galleys that made up the rest of his squadron fought the eight galleys commanded by Don Juan de Cardona. Luckily for Andrea Doria, the Marquis of Santa Cruz, who was in command of the Christian rearguard, came to his assistance.

To the right, Chulouk Bey of Alexandria, leader of Ali Pasha's Egyptian contingent, succeeded in turning the Holy League's left flank, sinking six galleys before determined Venetian resistance, as well as a mutiny among the Christian galley slaves on the Egyptian vessels and the timely arrival of a galleass, put an end to Chulouk Bey's attack. When he, too, was killed in the fighting, the Egyptians also turned and fled.

By 4.00 pm, the battle was over. Uluj Ali and his ships had managed to scuttle to safety, but they were all that was left of the once-proud Ottoman navy. Only 47 Ottoman galleys were able to disengage and make for home; 117 galleys had been captured by the Christians and around 25,000 Ottomans killed. The Christians lost 12 galleys and 7,000 men, but had freed 10,000 galley slaves. With the defeat at Lepanto, Ottoman naval dominance in the Mediterranean was at an end.

The Spanish Armada

IN A RUNNING NAVAL BATTLE UP THE ENGLISH CHANNEL FROM 31 JULY TO 9 AUGUST 1558, THE SUPPOSEDLY INVINCIBLE SPANISH ARMADA WAS EVENTUALLY DEFEATED AND PHILIP II'S PLAN TO INVADE ENGLAND FOILED.

Relations between Philip II of Spain and Elizabeth I had been cool for years, but, in the 1580s, they went from bad to worse. The raids launched on Spanish possessions and treasure ships in the New World by English privateers such as Sir Francis Drake and Sir John Hawkins were a constant thorn in Philip's side. Elizabeth's decision to assist the Dutch, who had rebelled against Spanish rule over the Netherlands, was another contributing factor, as was her decision to have Mary, Queen of Scots, executed for high treason in 1587. Not only was Mary a Catholic, but up until the time of her death she had been the heir apparent to the throne, since Elizabeth was unmarried and had no heirs.

In fact, Philip had begun preparations for launching what he christened 'the

> *Medina Sidonia was to steamroller his way up the English Channel, crushing Elizabeth's fleet en route and rendezvous with the Duke of Parma in command of an army...*

enterprise of England' two years before Mary's death. It took him far longer than he had anticipated to get the fleet ready for sea. The death of the Marquis of Santa Cruz, Philip's first choice as the Armada's commander, in February 1587 was one delaying factor; the pre-emptive raid Drake launched on Cadiz that April was another. Santa Cruz's replacement, the Duke of Medina Sidonia, had very little or no naval experience. His orders from Philip were explicit. Medina Sidonia was to steamroller his way up the English Channel, crushing Elizabeth's fleet as he went, and rendezvous with the Duke of Parma, who was in command of an army of Spanish veterans

The map shows the routes taken by the Spanish Armada and the English fleet towards and away from the site of battle in the English Channel.

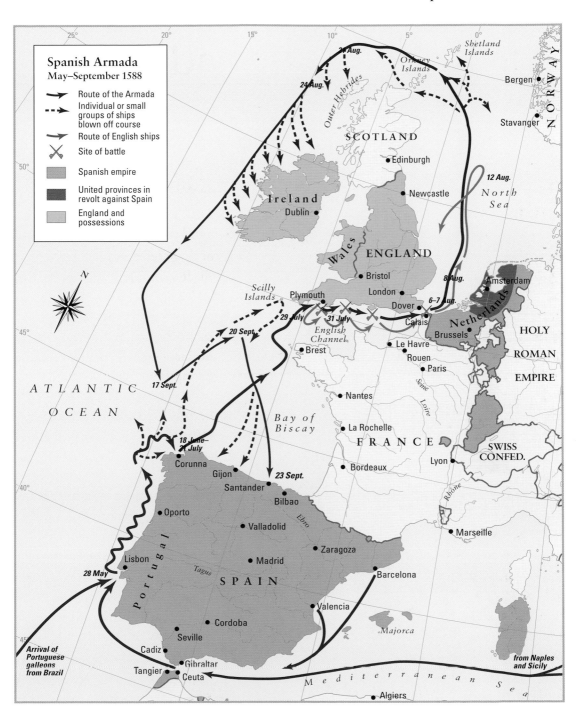

Spanish Armada
May–September 1588

→ Route of the Armada
⇢ Individual or small groups of ships blown off course
⇀ Route of English ships
✕ Site of battle
Spanish empire
United provinces in revolt against Spain
England and possessions

Shetland Islands

NORWAY
Bergen
Stavanger

Orkney Islands

Outer Hebrides

SCOTLAND
Edinburgh
Newcastle

North Sea

12 Aug.

Ireland
Dublin

Wales
ENGLAND
Bristol
London

8 Aug.
Amsterdam
Netherlands
6–7 Aug.
Dover
Calais
Brussels

31 July
29 July
Plymouth

English Channel
Brest
Le Havre
Rouen
Paris

Scilly Islands

ATLANTIC OCEAN

N

17 Sept.
20 Sept.

Bay of Biscay
Nantes
La Rochelle

FRANCE
Bordeaux
Lyon

HOLY ROMAN EMPIRE

SWISS CONFED.

18 June–21 July
Corunna
Gijon
Santander
Bilbao
23 Sept.

Oporto
Valladolid
Zaragoza
Marseille

Portugal
Lisbon
Madrid
Barcelona

Tagus
SPAIN
Valencia

28 May

Ebro

Arrival of Portuguese galleons from Brazil

Cordoba
Seville
Cadiz
Gibraltar
Tangier
Ceuta

Majorca

from Naples and Sicily

Mediterranean Sea
Algiers

Seine
Loire
Rhône

in Flanders. Medina Sidonia was to convoy Parma's army across the Channel to make a landing in the Thames estuary.

Privateer and great favourite of Elizabeth I, Sir Francis Drake made a fortune relieving Spanish ships of their New World gold.

FIGHTING UP THE CHANNEL

The Armada sailed from Lisbon on 28 May 1588. Unexpected storms and a shortage of drinking water forced it to put into the port of Corunna for a month. It was not until 29 July that, having sailed slowly across the Bay of Biscay, it entered the English Channel and was sighted off the Cornish coast. The news of its approach was promptly reported to Lord Howard of Effingham, the commander of Elizabeth's fleet, which had gathered at Plymouth ready for action.

The opening clash took place off Plymouth on 31 July, when Howard sailed 64 of his ships across the path of the Armada, which Medina Sidonia had formed into a huge crescent, spreading out for around 3 km (2 miles) from left to right. It was an imposing sight, but the English were not to be deterred. By adroit manoeuvring, Howard managed to position himself upwind of the Armada's crescent-shaped formation. Then his ships turned smartly and opened fire, aiming broadside after broadside at their foes. By employing hit-and-run tactics and relying on cannon fire to harass their opponents, the English denied the Spanish any chance to close with them and then board.

Frustrated by the English ability to avoid close combat, the Armada continued to progress up the Channel. By 2 August it was west of Portland Bill. Howard attacked again, only to be forced to break off action when his ships ran short of ammunition.

Medina Sidonia then decided to sail into the Solent to attempt to capture Portsmouth, but he abandoned the plan when Sir Francis Drake attacked him unexpectedly while Howard and Sir Martin Frobisher blocked the Solent's entrance. The Armada sailed on until it reached Calais, where it anchored off the port on 6 August 1558.

FACT FILE

Spanish Armada

Dates: 31 July–9 August 1558

Location: English Channel

Historical Context: A consequence of troubled relations between Elizabeth I of England and Philip II of Spain

States Involved: England; Spain

Commanders and Leaders: Lord Howard of Effingham, Sir Francis Drake (England); the Duke of Medina Sidonia, the Duke of Parma (Spain)

Outcome: Decisive English victory

Aftermath: The Spanish fleet lost its reputation for invincibility

'GOD BLEW AND THEY WERE SCATTERED'

Medina Sidonia had reached his objective. Parma had not. A messenger warned him that it would be a further six days before Parma could start embarking his army. In the meantime, Howard's fleet, reinforced by Lord Seymour's 35 ships from Dover, had dropped anchor nearby. At midnight on 8 August, Howard launched eight fireships to drift towards the Spanish. Though only six got through, the panic-stricken Spanish captains cut their anchor cables and scattered.

Howard had achieved his goal of breaking up Medina Sidonia's fleet, which was now strung out in packets in the shallow waters along the Flemish coast. As the admiral tried to reform the Armada off Gravelines, the English closed in for the kill. The battle lasted for nine hours. Ten Spanish ships were badly damaged; one was sunk. Medina Sidonia had had enough. Leading the Armada into the North Sea, he decided to sail round the British Isles and back to Spain. On the way, he lost at least 24 more ships, driven on to the Irish coast after encountering a near hurricane.

Philip tried to shrug off the defeat – in fact, he ordered preparations to be made for the despatch of a second Armada, but it never sailed. In any event, there was no disguising the extent of the English victory.

Breitenfeld

When Gustavus Adolphus, the king of Sweden, clashed with Count Tilly, leader of the armies of the Catholic League, during the Thirty Years' War, his stunning victory signalled the start of a military revolution.

After years of campaigning between Catholics and Protestants, it looked as though the religious war in Germany was turning in favour of the Catholics. Then, in July 1630, Gustavus Adolphus of Sweden entered the conflict. His motives were twofold – to save the German Protestant princes from defeat and, at the same time, to win control of the southern Baltic coast for his country.

Little was known about the Swedes and their military capabilities, which may go some way to explaining why, at least at first, Gustavus struggled to attract allies. Certainly Count Tilly, the commander of the Catholic League's army, did not regard the Swedish intervention as a serious threat. He elected to continue campaigning in northern Italy, rather than return to Germany to deal with his new foes. It was only in early 1631 that he began moving north again.

As Tilly's and Gustavus' forces began manoeuvring towards each other, one thing stood in their way. The Electorate of Saxony, which blocked both their paths, was neutral. When the emperor ordered

An engraving of Gustavus Adolphus of Sweden, who decided to enter the Thirty Years' War on the side of the German Protestant princes.

Tilly to invade it to punish John George, its ruler, for having refused an imperial order to disband his army, Gustavus found the ally he had been seeking.

THE ARMIES PREPARE

Linking up with the Saxons north of Leipzig, Gustavus advanced towards the city, which Tilly had captured on 15 September 1631. Learning of Gustavus' approach, Tilly debated what to do. As he was heavily outnumbered – he had 36,000 under him, while Gustavus and John George commanded 42,000 soldiers between them – common sense told him to wait for reinforcements.

Count Pappenheim, who commanded the Catholic cavalry, was eager to attack, however, and rode north with his troops to seek out the enemy. Having made contact with the Swedes on the evening of 16 September, he sent a messenger to Tilly to tell him that he was unable to withdraw. The reluctant Tilly was forced to march to Pappenheim's rescue.

The resulting battle was fought on a treeless plain just 8 km (5 miles) north of Leipzig. Tilly's army formed up on a ridge between the villages of Seehausen and Breitenfeld. His 14 Spanish-style *tercios* – bristling battle-squares of pikemen protected by small detachments of musketeers at the corners – were in

FACT FILE

Breitenfeld

Date: 17 September 1631

Historical Context: The Thirty Years' War (1618–1648)

States Involved: Holy Roman Empire; Sweden, Saxony

Commanders and Leaders: Count Tilly, Count Pappenheim, Count von Furstenberg (Holy Roman Empire); Gustavus Adolphus, General Johan Banér, General Gustav Horn, John George I, Hans Georg von Arnim-Boitzenburg, Robert Munro (Sweden/Saxony)

Outcome: Decisive Swedish victory

the centre. His cavalry, commanded by Pappenheim and Count von Furstenberg, were stationed to the left and right, and his artillery deployed in front of his infantry. Despite being outnumbered, the Catholic commander was confident that his veterans would win the day.

Gustavus delegated command of the Swedish right and left to generals Horn and Banér, while he took charge of the centre. He stationed the Saxons to his left. Instead of mimicking Tilly and forming a single battle line, the Swedes formed two lines. Unusually for the time, Gustavus also positioned musketeers among his cavalry,

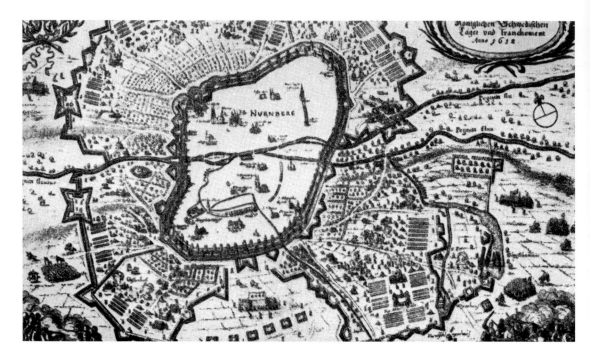

which was stationed on the Swedish flanks. These musketeers had been trained to fight in the cavalry's support.

An old engraving of the Swedish camp at the seige of Nuremberg in 1632, part of Gustavus' campaign during the Thirty Years' War.

GUSTAVUS TRIUMPHS

The battle started around noon with a two-hour exchange of artillery fire. Then Tilly took the initiative. Planning to outflank his opponents on both wings, he ordered Pappenheim and Furstenberg to attack. On the left, Pappenheim's cavalry swept around Banér's right to engage the Swedish cavalry reserve. The Swedes reacted by extending their line to counter the threat. Fierce fighting continued for around three hours until Pappenheim eventually fell

back. Things seemed to be going better for Tilly elsewhere on the battlefield. Soon after Pappenheim charged forwards, the *tercios* began to advance with more cavalry guarding their flanks.

To begin with, it looked as though Tilly was intending to strike directly at the Swedish left wing, but then the *tercios* suddenly veered to the right to attack the Saxons instead. Furstenberg's cavalry charged and swept round the Saxon flank. Taken by surprise, the Saxons turned and fled. The *tercios* now turned against Horn, whose flank was open to attack. Unlike the Saxons, however, Horn did not panic. Seeing that Tilly's troops were being slow to reorganize and their supporting cavalry was exposed, positioned between the Swedes and their own infantry, he threw every man he had into an immediate attack. The cavalry fell back in disorder on to their own infantry, causing total confusion in its ranks. The Swedes surged forwards, forcing the *tercios* back. Tilly was wounded and forced to leave the field. It was time for Gustavus to strike.

He marched into the gap that had opened in the Catholic centre, capturing Tilly's artillery, butchering five regiments that vainly tried to make a last stand and cutting the Leipzig road. Tilly's army broke and fled. The Protestants had gained a crucial victory, and Gustavus had won the day.

The movements of the Swedish and Imperial armies during the Battle of Breitenfeld.

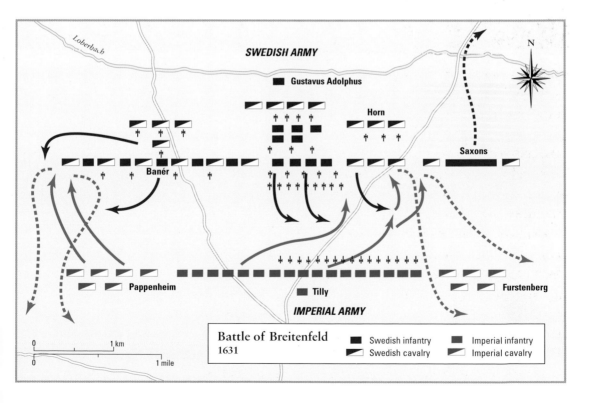

Battle of Breitenfeld
1631

Swedish infantry   Imperial infantry
Swedish cavalry   Imperial cavalry

Blenheim

MARLBOROUGH'S VICTORY OVER LOUIS XIV'S ARMIES IN AUGUST 1704 ESTABLISHED HIM AS ONE OF THE GREATEST COMMANDERS IN HISTORY. HIS TRIUMPH PUT AN END TO FRANCE'S REPUTATION FOR INVINCIBILITY ON THE BATTLEFIELD.

In 1704, two years after the outbreak of the War of the Spanish Succession between France, Austria, England and the Netherlands, the French king Louis XIV decided on an audacious move to bring the conflict to a triumphant conclusion. In alliance with Maximilian II of Bavaria, he resolved to attack Vienna, the Austrian capital. If the city fell, Louis believed that the coalition opposing him would collapse like a house of cards. As a result, France would establish its hegemony over continental Europe once and for all.

Emperor Leopold I was well aware of the French threat. He hastily recalled Prince Eugene of Savoy and his army from Italy, while at the same time calling on his English and Dutch allies for help. Marlborough, who had been in command of the Anglo-Dutch army in the Netherlands since the outbreak of war, was anxious to march to Leopold's assistance, but the Dutch were reluctant to cooperate. They feared that any such move would leave their own country exposed to a French attack.

Marlborough promised the Dutch that he would advance only as far as the river Moselle, but he had no intention of keeping his word. Instead, he moved south along the Rhine and onwards as far as the town of Donauwörth, which he captured after a lightning attack on the Schellenberg, the fortress the Bavarians had hastily erected to protect the town.

Securing this vital river crossing enabled Marlborough to continue his advance across the Danube. His plan was to position his army between the Franco-Bavarians and the Austrian capital.

Leopold I hastily recalled Prince Eugene of Savoy and his army from Italy, while at the same time calling on his English and Dutch allies for help.

TAKEN BY SURPRISE

The whole march took Marlborough just five weeks to complete. Reinforced by Prince Eugene, he prepared to confront the Franco-Bavarian army, with Marshal Tallard now in overall command. Tallard had taken up position just west of the small village of Blenheim, along the banks of the Danube. The Franco-Bavarian line stretched 6.5 km (4 miles) north from the Danube towards the hills and woods of the Swabian Jura. It was anchored on the villages of Lutzingen to the left, Oberglau in the centre and Blenheim itself on the right. Tallard ordered the Bavarians to take

The map below illustrates Marlborough's tactics at the Battle of Blenheim.

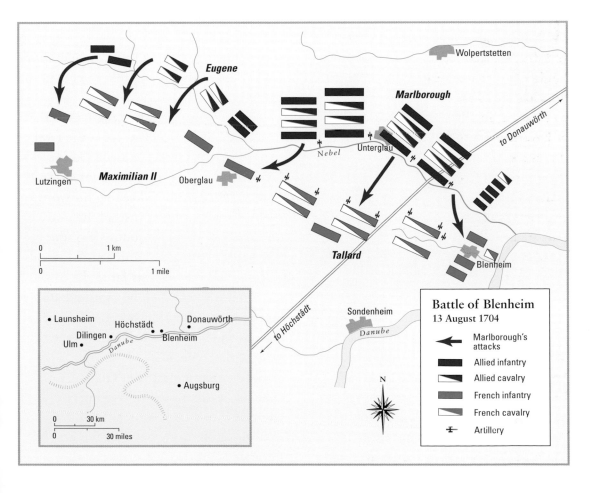

up position around Lutzingen, while he and Marshal Marsin concentrated their French troops on the villages of Blenheim and Oberglau respectively. Tallard was confident that the position they had taken up was impregnable.

Marlborough resolved on an immediate attack despite being outnumbered – he had 56,000 troops under his command, opposing Franco-Bavarian troops

numbering at least 60,000. At 2.00 am on 13 August 1704, his forces began to advance westwards, reaching high ground at Wolperstetten some four hours later. As the early morning mist began to lift, the Franco-Bavarians discovered much to their amazement that Marlborough's entire army was now within a stone's throw of their positions.

A GLORIOUS VICTORY

The battle began at 8.30 am, when the French artillery opened fire. Marlborough's cannon promptly replied. Out of necessity Tallard's battle plan was simple – he had been taken completely by surprise. His anticipation was that Marlborough would advance across the river Nebel. If he did so, he would be caught in a crossfire from Oberglau and Blenheim. Tallard would then counter-attack and drive Marlborough's men into the surrounding marshland.

Marlborough was not to be duped. Realizing that the enemy's right was stronger than its left, he broke with military convention by choosing to attack the stronger, not the weaker flank. While Prince Eugene and his Austrians attacked the Bavarians at Lutzingen, Lord John Cutts' column was ordered across the Nebel and then to attack Blenheim itself. Though the French beat back the initial

An engraving of John Churchill, 1st Duke of Marlborough (1650–1722), whose reputation as a great military commander was gained at Blenheim.

assaults, their commander panicked. Without consulting Tallard, he ordered all available French reserves into the village. It was a colossal mistake. 'The men were now so crowded in upon one another', wrote one observer, 'that they could not even fire, let alone receive or carry out any orders'. Marlborough ordered Cutts to keep the French pinned down.

What Marlborough was waiting for was the news that Prince Eugene's attack had succeeded. Eventually it came, together with the tidings that the French were pinned down in Oberglau as well. Marlborough promptly ordered the bulk of his army across the Nebel. Tallard had only nine fresh battalions left to oppose him.

As the early morning mist began to lift, the Franco-Bavarians discovered to their amazement that Marlborough's army was now within a stone's throw...

At around 5.00 pm, Marlborough struck at Tallard. The French cavalry was the first to be routed; then the infantry was slaughtered while vainly trying to form squares. Tallard's line broke, and joined by the Bavarians, the French began to flee from the battlefield. The French troops trapped in Blenheim held out until 9.00 pm, when over 10,000 of them surrendered. Tallard himself was among the prisoners. It was a triumph for the Duke of Marlborough and his risky strategy.

FACT FILE

Blenheim

Date: 13 August 1704

Location: Along the banks of the Danube, just west of Blenheim

Historical Context: The War of the Spanish Succession (1702–1713)

States Involved: England, Holy Roman Empire; France, Electorate of Bavaria

Commanders and Leaders: Duke of Marlborough, Prince Eugene of Savoy (England/Holy Roman Empire); Marshal Tallard, Marshal Marsin, Maximilian II Emanuel (Franco-Bavarians)

Outcome: Decisive victory for England and the Holy Roman Empire

Aftermath: Established Marlborough as one of the greatest commanders in history; put an end to France's reputation for invincibility on the battlefield

Poltava

TSAR **P**ETER THE **G**REAT'S CRUSHING DEFEAT OF **C**HARLES **XII**'S INVADING ARMY
IN **J**ULY **1709** SIGNALLED THE END OF **S**WEDISH MILITARY DOMINANCE AND THE
EMERGENCE OF **R**USSIA AS ONE OF THE GREAT **E**UROPEAN POWERS.

As Russia and Sweden battled it out for Baltic supremacy in the Great Northern War, Charles XII of Sweden devised an audacious plan to bring the conflict to a triumphant conclusion. In 1708, he embarked on an invasion of Russia. A few years before, such an invasion might well have been successful; earlier in the war, Charles' forces had inflicted multiple defeats on the badly led, ill-trained and ill-equipped Russians. Now, things were very different. Peter the Great had learnt from his defeats and reorganized his army along modern European lines. Launching such an attack now was the greatest gamble of Charles' turbulent career.

> *Charles turned down his generals' advice to fall back. Instead he ordered them to prepare to resume the advance with the aim of... finally taking Moscow.*

PRELUDE TO POLTAVA

Advancing from Lithuania, Charles got as far as Smolensk before turning south for the Ukraine, where he planned to spend the winter. He also hoped to find allies among the Cossacks – Ivan Mazeppa, the leader of the Hetman Cossacks, had promised the Swedes his support – but, in the event, only the Zaporozhian Cossacks rallied to the Swedish cause. Nor did the reinforcements Charles had been counting on manage to join him in time. Peter defeated Charles and his allies at the Battle of Lesnaia that September.

Charles remained undaunted, even though his army suffered terribly in the face of the rigours of the harsh Russian winter. He turned down his generals' advice to fall back. Instead, he ordered them to prepare to resume the advance

The map shows the movements of the Swedish and Russian forces during the Battle of Poltava.

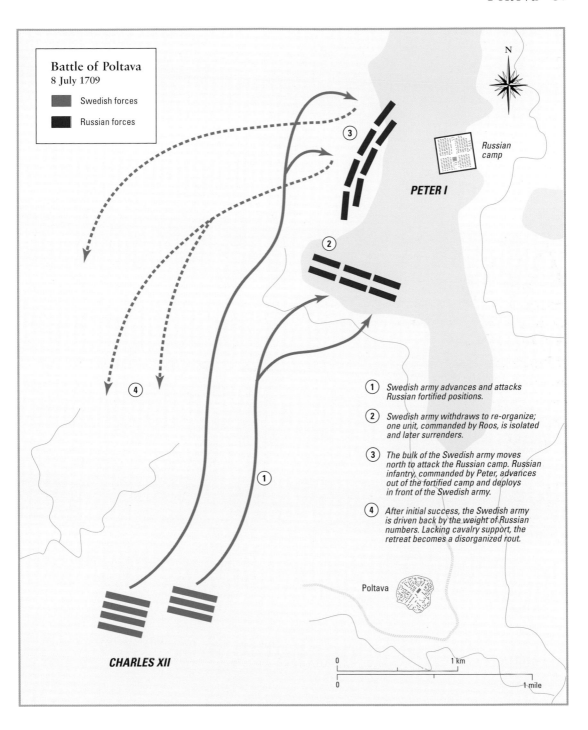

Battle of Poltava
8 July 1709

Swedish forces

Russian forces

N

Russian camp

PETER I

① Swedish army advances and attacks Russian fortified positions.

② Swedish army withdraws to re-organize; one unit, commanded by Roos, is isolated and later surrenders.

③ The bulk of the Swedish army moves north to attack the Russian camp. Russian infantry, commanded by Peter, advances out of the fortified camp and deploys in front of the Swedish army.

④ After initial success, the Swedish army is driven back by the weight of Russian numbers. Lacking cavalry support, the retreat becomes a disorganized rout.

Poltava

CHARLES XII

0 _____ 1 km

0 _____ 1 mile

with the aim of capturing Kharkov and Kursk, and finally taking Moscow. As a first step, this involved getting the Swedish army across the river Vorskla. In May 1709, Charles accordingly began to besiege Poltava, the town controlling the best crossing point.

The Swedes needed to take Poltava quickly, but the garrison managed to hold out until 4 June when Peter's army arrived on the scene. Estimates vary as to exactly how many men Peter had under his command; all that is certain is that they vastly outnumbered the Swedes.

An engraving of the Battle of Poltava, showing Peter the Great on horseback in the midst of the conflict.

THE WOUNDED KING

Peter positioned his army in an entrenched camp on a low ridge with forests on two sides of it and the river Vorskla behind it. Additionally, he set his troops to work to build a chain of ten redoubts to defend the only open approach from the south. His plan was to remain on the defensive. If the impetuous Charles attacked the Russian position, so much the better.

Charles, however, was no longer in a position to exercise direct command over his forces. On 25 June, he was badly wounded in the foot while carrying out a reconnaissance and was forced to delegate authority to Field Marshal Rehnskjold, who, though a veteran of many campaigns, was not as inspiring a leader. He and General Lewenhaupt, one of his fellow commanders, again counselled retreat, but Charles was in no mood to listen. On 7 July Charles ordered Rehnskjold to launch an all-out attack on Peter's position the very next day. To make sure that his orders were carried out, he told the reluctant Rehnskjold that he would be carried into battle on a litter to watch the action.

BOLDNESS LEADS TO DISASTER

Rehnskjold put 18 battalions of infantry and 12 squadrons of cavalry into the field. His plan was to rush the outlying Russian redoubts, rout the Russian cavalry and then storm Peter's camp. Unfortunately for the Swedes, their key generals were at loggerheads; Rehnskjold disliked Lewenhaupt so much that he had not even bothered to inform him of his intentions. He kept the other Swedish generals almost as much in the dark.

The attack started at dawn. As the Swedes advanced, they were met by the Russian cavalry, which threw them back. The Swedish cavalry counter-attacked, only to be dispersed by heavy Russian fire. Rehnskjold then ordered the infantry forwards again. Although they succeeded in capturing two of the Russian redoubts, the others held firm against them. Even worse, General Roos' troops managed to become pinned down among the redoubts. Roos was surrounded by the Russians and forced to surrender.

In the meantime, the rest of the Swedish infantry had moved further forwards and was preparing to launch a frontal attack on the entrenchments of the Russian camp. Pounded by Peter's artillery, the Swedes charged, only to be confronted by the Russian infantry. They were forced back with heavy losses. Then, the Russian right wing swung forwards to flank the Swedes. They broke and began to flee the field in disarray.

Charles and 1,500 of his troops managed to reach neutral Turkey and safety. Lewenhaupt was not as lucky. He and the 14,000 men he had managed to salvage from the disaster were trapped by the pursuing Russians on the river Dnieper. On 11 July 1709, they too were compelled to surrender. Peter's victory at Poltava marked the emergence of Russia as a great European power.

FACT FILE
Poltava

Dates: 8 July 1709

Location: Poltava, Ukraine

Historical Context: The Great Northern War (1700–1721)

States Involved: Russia; Sweden

Commanders and Leaders: Charles XII, Carl Gustaf Rehnskjold (Sweden); Peter I, Alexander Mehnshikov (Russia)

Outcome: Decisive Russian victory

Aftermath: Peter's victory signalled the end of Swedish military dominance, and Russia emerged as a great European power

Plassey

ROBERT CLIVE'S DEFEAT OF SIRAJ-UD-DAULAH, THE NAWAB OF BENGAL, PAVED THE WAY FOR ESTABLISHING BRITISH RULE OVER THE WHOLE OF INDIA. IT WAS A VICTORY ACHIEVED AS MUCH BY BRIBERY AS BY PROWESS ON THE BATTLEFIELD.

The Seven Years' War, fought between 1756 and 1763, was the first truly global conflict in history. While fighting raged in Europe and North America – where the conflict was known as the French and Indian War – it also spread to the more outlying parts of the British and French empires.

In India, fighting began in Bengal in 1756, when the British East India Company began reinforcing its trading posts there. Siraj-ud-Daulah, the 23-year-old prince who had just succeeded to the throne as nawab, ordered them to cease their preparations for war. The East India Company ignored the request.

In reprisal, the nawab ordered his army to attack Fort William, the East India Company's stronghold in Calcutta, the most important trading centre in India. Following its fall that June, the nawab allegedly ordered 146 of his European prisoners to be incarcerated in a tiny cell in the fort. The following morning, only 23 were left alive. The rest had suffocated or had been crushed to death.

REGAINING CALCUTTA

News of the fall of Calcutta and the horrors of the so-called 'Black Hole' did not reach Madras, where the East India Company had its headquarters, until mid-July. The British readied a response. Though it took time to assemble the necessary forces, Robert Clive and his troops eventually were despatched on board four ships-of-the-line, commanded by Vice-Admiral Charles Watson, to retake the city of Calcutta.

Clive already had a formidable military reputation, thanks to the brilliant leadership he had displayed when besieged at Arcot for 50 days in 1751. William Pitt the Elder praised him as a 'heaven-born general'. With 900 British regulars and 1,500 sepoys, he reached the river Hooghly in late December, rescued the surviving prisoners and recaptured the city.

He met only token resistance, as, on the news of the British approach, the nawab's 500-strong garrison fled in disarray.

Clive pressed forwards. On 9 January 1757, his forces stormed Hooghly, 37 km (23 miles) to the north of Calcutta. The nawab marched from his capital to confront him, arriving outside the city on 3 February. The following morning, taking advantage of a thick fog, Clive struck at the nawab's camp. The attack, although not decisive, was enough to scare the nawab into coming to terms. On 5 February, he signed a peace treaty that gave the East India Company back everything it had lost in the previous skirmishing.

Clive now planned to attack the French at Chandernagar, but, before doing so, he sought an assurance that the nawab would remain neutral. He interpreted the evasive reply he received as tacit consent. On 14 March 1757, he attacked. The French held out for ten days before surrendering.

Infuriated by the British attack, the nawab planned revenge. For his part, Clive now distrusted the Bengali ruler completely, especially when his spies discovered that Siraj-ud-Daulah was intriguing with the French. He decided to back the faction at the nawab's court that was already plotting his overthrow. Mir Jafar, one of the most important commanders in the nawab's army, was the leader of the conspiracy. Clive promised to put him on the throne if he turned against his master.

The stage was set for a final confrontation. Clive ordered all his forces to concentrate at Chandernagar in readiness for a march on Murshidabad, the nawab's capital. On 22 June, he reached

Battle of Plassey 1757

(1) The Nawab of Bengal attacks the British, who are located in a grove. The attack is repelled.

(2) Further attacks follow, supported by artillery, which are again repelled.

(3) The British launch an attack after a rainstorm; with their powder wet, the Bengalis fall back.

The movements of the two armies between the Bengali and British camps during the Battle of Plassey.

Plassey, setting up camp about 1.5 km (1 mile) from the entrenchments where the nawab had concentrated his entire army.

VICTORY AT PLASSEY

The next day, the battle began with a fierce artillery barrage. Both sides kept up fire for three hours, but to relatively little effect. Then nature took a hand. It was the monsoon season and a fierce rainstorm suddenly broke over the battlefield. Clive's troops used tarpaulins to shelter their weapons; their enemies were not so careful. They were thus forced to slacken their rate of fire, while Clive's gunners kept up their relentless cannonade, dispersing the Bengali attempt at a cavalry charge.

Once the storm had cleared, the nawab's men started to stream back towards their entrenchments. It was Colonel Clive's moment to attack. With their muskets rendered useless by the rain, the Bengali retreat soon turned into a rout. Mir Jafar earned his bribe by refusing to let the division he commanded take part in the fighting that followed.

For his part, the nawab, who had already hastened back to Murshidabad, fled the city in disguise, hoping to reach safety in Patna. Mir Jafar's men overtook him on 2 July – the day Clive declared the nawab officially deposed – and murdered him the same night.

Historical engraving showing British troops in India defending themselves against Indian attack during one of the conflicts of the period.

FACT FILE

Plassey

Date: 23 June 1757

Location: Plassey, Bengal

Historical Context: Seven Years' War (1756–1763)

States Involved: British East India Company; Nawab of Bengal

Commanders and Leaders: Colonel Robert Clive, Vice-Admiral Charles Watson, Major Grant, Major Eyre Coot, Captain Gaupp (British East India Company); Mohan Lal, Mir Madan, Mir Jafar Ali Khan, Nawab Siraj-ud-Daulah, Yar Lutuf Khan, Monsieur Sinfray (Nawab of Bengal)

Outcome: Decisive victory for the British East India Company

Aftermath: Paved the way for establishing British rule over the whole of India

Quebec

THE FALL OF QUEBEC IN 1759 WAS THE TURNING POINT IN BRITAIN'S STRUGGLE TO WREST CONTROL OF CANADA FROM FRANCE. UNFORTUNATELY, THEIR COMMANDER, THE 32-YEAR-OLD JAMES WOLFE, WAS KILLED IN THE MOMENT OF VICTORY.

Fighting in the French and Indian War – the name given to the Seven Years' War in North America – actually started two years before that conflict broke out in Europe, when Britain and France formally went to war. In North America, the French had the upper hand at first, but in 1758, the British successfully took the offensive. Their capture of Louisbourg in July gave them command of the Gulf of St Lawrence and opened the way for an attack on French Canada.

Command of the third expedition was entrusted to Major-General James Wolfe, who, at 32, was one of the youngest and most controversial of the British commanders.

ATTACKING QUEBEC

William Pitt the Elder, the British prime minister at the time, was the mastermind behind the drive to force the French out of their Canadian possessions. In 1759, he ordered expeditions to be mounted against Fort Niagara, Fort Ticanderoga and Quebec, which dominated the St Lawrence River. Command of the third expedition was entrusted to Major-General James Wolfe, who, at the age of 32, was one of the youngest and most controversial of the British commanders. The Duke of Newcastle was one of those who warned George II against promoting him. George replied testily: 'Mad, is he? Then I hope he will bite some of my other generals!' The promotion went ahead.

On 26 June 1759, Wolfe's troops arrived off the city of Quebec – they had been transported up the St Lawrence by Admiral Sir Charles Saunders and his fleet – and landed on the Ile d'Orléans and the south bank of the river. The landings took the French commander, the Marquis de Montcalm, by surprise, since he had anticipated a British thrust from an entirely different direction.

Nevertheless, he was quick to react to the new threat. Concentrating the bulk of his forces at Beauport, to the east of the city, he began throwing up fortifications along the northern shore of the St Lawrence to thwart any attempt Wolfe might make to force his way across.

A DARING PLAN

Wolfe's first move was to start bombarding the city, while ships from Sanders' fleet ran

Battle of Quebec 1759

1. The battle is fought on the vast Plains of Abraham outside the city.

2. After a few hours the British win the battle. James Wolfe, their leader, falls on the field. Montcalm, the French commander, is mortally wounded and dies in Quebec a few hours later.

the gauntlet of French counter-battery fire in order to make their way upstream to reconnoitre other possible landing places. Then, on 31 July, he attacked the French at Beauport. The assault was a failure.

The British commander changed tactics. He despatched troops upstream to threaten the French supply lines to Montreal. Montcalm reacted by detaching 3,000 men from his main force to check any possible incursion. Meanwhile, Wolfe set about planning a further landing. On 10 September, he told his commanders that he and 4,000 troops would cross the St Lawrence by night to land at the Anse de Foulon, a cove to the south-west of Quebec where a steep, narrow path had been discovered leading up to the Heights of Abraham above the city. While he and his men were scrambling up the path in the middle of the night, the rest of the British forces would launch a diversionary attack against Beauport.

THE ATTACK BEGINS

It was a bold plan and it succeeded to a marvel. At around midnight on 12 September 1759, Wolfe made his way cautiously across the river. The small militia detachment of French troops

The map shows the British advancing towards the French during the Battle of Quebec.

positioned to watch over the cove was speedily overwhelmed, though not before its commander had managed to despatch a messenger to Montcalm, alerting him to Wolfe's landing. Distracted by the British feint at Beauport, the French commander took time to react. When he did, he responded decisively. Without waiting for the troops he had detached to rejoin him, he headed west, determined to attack Wolfe before he could establish himself on the Heights.

Part of the historic fortifications that remain on the Plains of Abraham, this Martello tower overlooks the St Lawrence River.

A TEN-MINUTE BATTLE

The resulting clash lasted barely ten minutes. The British, who had deployed in line in two-deep ranks rather than the customary three, held their fire until the advancing French columns were little more than a few metres away. Then the first rank fired a devastating volley; advancing a few paces, the second rank opened fire to similar effect. The shattered French formations immediately began to fall back in disorder.

As the battle ended, Montcalm was mortally wounded. Carried back to Quebec, he died the following day. Wolfe had already fallen. Early in the battle, he was shot in the wrist. Bandaging the wound, he continued forwards with his men, only to be shot in the stomach and chest. He died while issuing his final orders for his troops to press home their advance.

The British triumph was complete. The reinforcements Montcalm had summoned from Cap Rouge declined to attack when they arrived; similarly, Governor Pierre de Vendreuil, in charge of the defences at Beauport, decided to evacuate his positions and abandon the city.

Quebec was left open to the British. On 18 September, Jean-Baptiste Nicolas Roch de Ramezay, the commander of the garrison, surrendered. The fate of New France was sealed.

FACT FILE
Battle of Quebec

Date: 13 September 1759

Location: Quebec City

Historical Context: The French and Indian War (1754–63)

States Involved: Great Britain; France

Commanders and Leaders: James Wolfe, George Townshend (Great Britain); Louis-Joseph de Montcalm (France)

Outcome: Decisive British victory

Aftermath: The turning point in Britain's struggle to wrest control of Canada from France

Saratoga

WHEN HORATIO GATES FORCED MAJOR-GENERAL BURGOYNE TO SURRENDER AT SARATOGA, THE VICTORY WAS THE TURNING POINT IN THE WAR OF INDEPENDENCE. IT PERSUADED THE FRENCH TO ENTER THE WAR ON THE SIDE OF THE AMERICANS.

The campaign that led to disaster for the British in America had its roots in Britain's determination to put an end to the War of Independence once and for all. The result of the two battles they fought outside Saratoga in the early autumn of 1777 and Major-General John Burgoyne's subsequent surrender were the culmination of this campaign. The idea was to launch a three-pronged attack to gain control of upstate New York, so cutting off New England, 'the head of the rebellion', from the rest of the colonies. Burgoyne was the leading advocate of the plan.

What Burgoyne proposed found favour with the government in London and preparations were soon underway to launch the master stroke the British believed would win them the war. Burgoyne himself would transport his army by boat across

...the plan contained a major flaw. Because Burgoyne was junior in rank to Howe, he could not give him direct orders ... the necessary instructions were never despatched.

Lake Champlain from Quebec, capture Fort Ticonderoga and press on down the Hudson River to rendezvous at Albany with a second force, led by Colonel Barry St Leger, which would advance east from Lake Ontario and up the Mohawk River. In the meantime, General William Howe would move up the Hudson from New York, tying up any American troops that otherwise might be detached to check Burgoyne's advance.

Right at the start, the plan contained a major flaw. Because Burgoyne was junior in rank to Howe, he could not give him direct orders. The responsibility for doing this passed to Lord George Germain, the Secretary of State for the Colonies. For some unknown reason – some say it was due to incompetence and others to a secretarial oversight – the necessary instructions were never despatched. In ignorance of Burgoyne's intentions, Howe pressed ahead with his own plan to capture Philadelphia. His failure to link up with Burgoyne was a major factor in precipitating the latter's defeat.

FROM SUCCESS TO DISASTER

In the beginning, things went reasonably well for Burgoyne. On 6 July, Fort Ticonderoga fell, virtually without a shot being fired. However, Burgoyne's plan soon started to unravel. Harassed continually by the Americans as they continued their march southwards, it took Burgoyne's men almost a month to reach Fort Edward on the river Hudson. By this time they were starting to run short of food, ammunition and other essentials.

Burgoyne ordered a halt while a column of his German mercenaries was sent into Vermont for supplies. On 16 August, the Germans were defeated by the Americans at Bennington. St Leger was not doing much better. He had halted his advance to besiege Fort Stanwix and then, confronted by an American relieving force, had been forced to turn back to Fort Oswego. As this was not enough for the increasingly harassed Burgoyne, he now learnt that Howe, though he had left New York, was marching on Philadelphia, not up the Hudson Valley as Burgoyne had confidently expected. Though Major-General Sir Henry Clinton, Howe's deputy, raided up the Hudson with what troops he had available, by the nature of things this could be little more than a diversion.

THE DECISIVE BATTLES

The hapless Burgoyne was left to struggle on unaided. He crossed the Hudson and continued to march south in a final effort to take Albany before the onset of winter. At Freeman's Farm on 19 September, he was confronted by General Horatio Gates, the newly appointed commander of the main American army in the north. Though the resulting battle was notionally

Historic Fort Ticonderoga, which initially fell to the British with hardly a shot being fired.

a draw, Burgoyne paid a heavy price for the stalemate. He lost twice as many men as his opponents. Nevertheless, he decided to launch another attack on 7 October – this time on the left of the American position on Bemis Heights, which commanded the Hudson and the road to Albany.

The attack started as what Burgoyne termed a reconnaissance in force, but soon escalated. Led by Brigadier-General Simon Fraser, the British advanced, only to run into vastly superior American forces. With his line collapsing, Fraser tried to rally his men, but was shot down and killed outright. The British were driven back, losing the two redoubts they had held at the start of the battle.

Leaving their wounded behind on the battlefield, the British fell back into Saratoga itself. Burgoyne hastily summoned a council of war. His army's supplies were now exhausted and he was left with two stark choices – to fight his way north to Fort Edward or to surrender. Though most of his officers were in favour of fighting on, Burgoyne decided on the second alternative. On 17 October he and the 5,791 men still under his command surrendered to Gates. The Americans had scored their first decisive victory.

The map illustrates the movements of the British and American armies during the Saratoga Campaign.

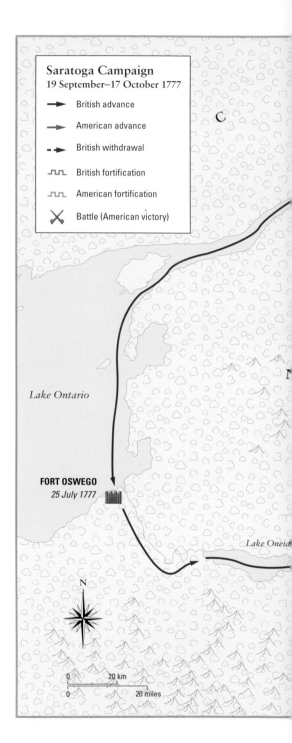

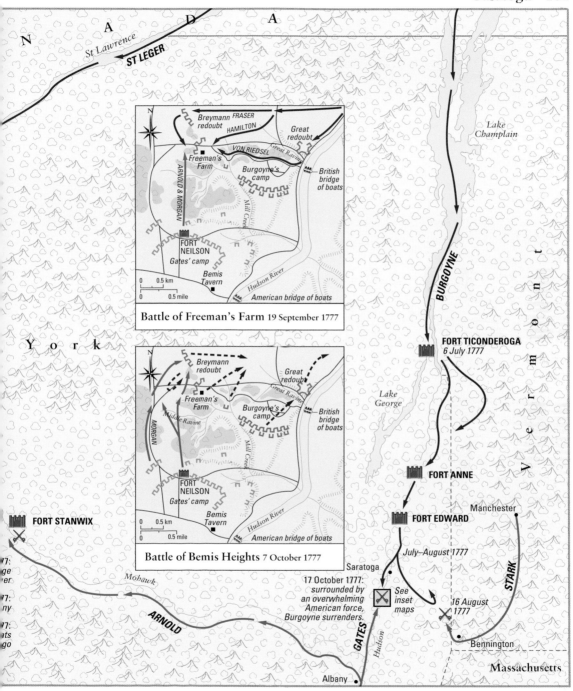

Battle of Freeman's Farm 19 September 1777

Battle of Bemis Heights 7 October 1777

Yorktown

WHEN LORD CORNWALLIS SURRENDERED TO GEORGE WASHINGTON IN OCTOBER 1781, THE AMERICAN WAR OF INDEPENDENCE EFFECTIVELY CAME TO AN END, ALTHOUGH IT TOOK ANOTHER TWO YEARS TO SIGN PEACE TERMS.

The disaster that overtook Lord Cornwallis and his army in Virginia in October 1781 was decisive in determining which side was ultimately victorious in the American War of Independence. Although substantial British forces remained active after Cornwallis' humiliating capitulation, his defeat finally broke the British government's resolve.

As 1781 dawned, however, it was the British, not the Americans, who were confident of ultimate success. The so-called 'southern strategy', devised by General Sir Henry Clinton, the recently appointed commander-in-chief, seemed to be winning the war. In 1778, Clinton had captured Savannah; the following year, he had defeated a joint French and American attempt to retake the city. In May 1780, he had forced Charleston – the South's largest city and most important seaport – to capitulate. It was the greatest British victory of the war.

Cornwallis, whom Clinton had appointed to take over from him in command in the South, carried on from where his predecessor had left off. Following a victory at Camden that August, he marched into North Carolina. Finally, in January 1781, Benedict Arnold, the turncoat general who had deserted the Americans to join the British, landed in Virginia. Meeting little or no resistance, he captured Richmond, the state capital, in 48 hours.

THE TIDE TURNS

Although it seemed as if the British were unstoppable, the tide of war was turning against them. In South Carolina, the Americans scored a victory over Banastre Tarleton; and in North Carolina, Cornwallis' troops were being harassed by relentless guerrilla attacks. Although Cornwallis won a last victory at Guildford Court House that March, it cost him a quarter of his men.

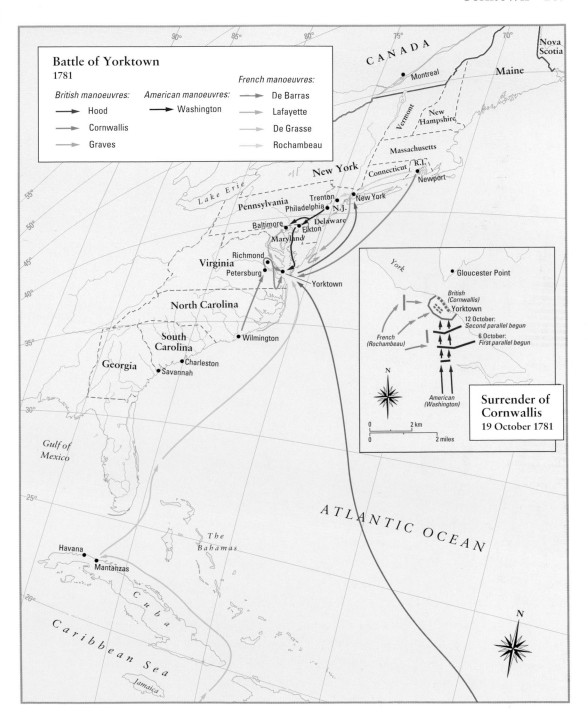

Battle of Yorktown
1781

British manoeuvres:
→ Hood
→ Cornwallis
→ Graves

American manoeuvres:
→ Washington

French manoeuvres:
→ De Barras
→ Lafayette
→ De Grasse
→ Rochambeau

Surrender of Cornwallis
19 October 1781

British (Cornwallis)
Yorktown
12 October: Second parallel begun
6 October: First parallel begun

French (Rochambeau)

American (Washington)

Gloucester Point

York

0   2 km
0   2 miles

N

Historic cannons at Yorktown overlooking the York river; the defeat of the British at Yorktown by Washington and his French allies was a defining moment in the battle for independence. General Cornwallis and his men laid down their arms and surrendered at Yorktown on 17 October 1781.

Cornwallis made a momentous decision to fall back from the Carolinas and strike into Virginia, but failed to inform Clinton of his intentions. Rather than applauding Cornwallis for his boldness, Clinton ordered him to march to the Virginia coast and ready his army to be transported by sea back to New York. Cornwallis accordingly moved to Yorktown on Chesapeake Bay. With its back to the sea and its supplies running low, his army was a tempting target for attack.

WASHINGTON STRIKES

It was the French who persuaded George Washington, the commander-in-chief of the Continental Army, that rather than trying to recapture New York, he would stand more chance of success by attacking Cornwallis. At first, Washington was reluctant to take the French advice; it took a threat from Admiral de Grasse to withdraw his fleet from American waters to get him to change his mind. When he did, he acted swiftly.

Leaving half the Continental Army behind to contain Clinton, Washington and de Rochambeau, the commander of the French expeditionary corps, moved swiftly south to attack Cornwallis, who was soon cut off by sea as well as by land. As the troops neared their objective, de Grasse forced Admiral Graves and his relieving squadron to turn back to New York.

Cornwallis had the advantage of being positioned behind strong defences. Washington's aim was to get within cannon range of them, sap his way forwards, bring up his heavy artillery and begin his siege. By 6 October, his sappers were ready to open their first parallel; three days later, his siege guns opened fire.

Soon, the shelling became constant, inflicting heavy damage on the defences. On 12 October, the sappers were able to start their second parallel, but they hit a snag. The trench could not be completed at its eastern end because it was vulnerable to fire from two British redoubts. Washington decided to attack and take them.

To distract Cornwallis, Washington launched two diversionary attacks before the main assault began. Under cover of darkness, the Americans took one redoubt at bayonet point, while French detachments captured the other. The twin success meant that Washington could move his heavy cannon even closer to the already-battered British fortifications.

'THE WORLD TURNED UPSIDE DOWN'

Cornwallis made a last attempt to avert disaster. He tried to move his remaining troops across the York River to attempt a breakout, but, with only a quarter of his men across, a sudden violent storm forced him to abandon the plan. He decided he had no alternative but to capitulate. At 10.00 am on 17 October, a British drummer beat out a request for a parley. Two days of negotiation followed, at the end of which the surrender was signed.

That afternoon Cornwallis' surviving troops, resplendent in new redcoats issued for the occasion, marched out to lay down their arms. As they did so, a British band struck up a march. It was the aptly titled 'The World Turned Upside Down', which was precisely what had happened. The siege was at an end. So, effectively, was the war and the British stranglehold on the North American continent. The balance of power had shifted irrevocably.

To distract Cornwallis, Washington launched two diversionary attacks before the main assault began. Under cover of darkness, the Americans took one redoubt...

Nineteenth Century

Napoleon, nationalism and the Industrial Revolution all combined to transform the face of warfare in the 19th century. By the end of the 1800s, it was clear that any future war would be more costly than ever before.

Marengo

NAPOLEON'S WIZARDRY IN SNATCHING VICTORY OUT OF THE JAWS OF DEFEAT WAS NEVER BETTER DISPLAYED THAN AT MARENGO IN 1800. AT THE END OF THE INITIAL FIGHTING, THE AUSTRIANS WERE CONVINCED THEY HAD WON THE BATTLE.

In spring 1800, with France once again at war with Austria and the powers allied with her in the Second Coalition, Napoleon, now First Consul, led an army across the Alps and into Italy. His primary aim was to raise the Austrian siege of Genoa, but, as it turned out, the city fell before he could relieve it. Nevertheless, Napoleon was still spoiling for a fight. Through skilful manoeuvring, he positioned his army so that it threatened the enemy lines of communication. The Austrians were left with two choices – either to attack the French or retreat.

When no Austrian challenge materialized, Napoleon was convinced that General Michael von Melas, the 70-year-old Austrian commander, had chosen the second alternative. Accordingly, he dispersed his forces to block all the possible escape routes he thought that the Austrians might take as they fell back on Genoa. Little did he realize that, far

from retreating, Melas was preparing to attack. His chosen battleground was near Marengo, a small village on the northern Italian plain not far from the city of Alessandria in Piedmont.

THE AUSTRIANS ATTACK

The battle began around mid-morning on 14 June 1800, when the Austrian advance guard engaged Lieutenant-General Claude Victor Perrin's infantry, which had been deployed in a defensive line along Fontanone Creek with units of French heavy cavalry to its left. As the Austrian attacks increased in intensity with the arrival of the bulk of the army on the field, Victor, now joined by Marshal Lannes, slowly began to fall back, with both commanders fighting stubbornly for every inch of ground as they retired.

As morning turned to afternoon, the French withdrew to new positions in the vineyards to the east of Marengo. It was

An engraving shows the death of General Desaix at the battle of Marengo. A favourite of Napoleon, he was killed just at the moment of victory.

now that Napoleon, who had dismissed the attack as nothing more than an Austrian feint to cover their withdrawal, finally arrived on the scene. He recalled the two infantry divisions he had detached from the army. Only one of them was close enough to be able to return in time to take part in the action and even then it would take it some hours to arrive on the scene. To buy time for Victor and Lannes' battle-weary troops to fall back, Napoleon threw all the fresh infantry he could muster into the yawning gaps that were opening up in the French battle-line. He then ordered a further withdrawal – this time to a position just west of San Giuliano.

A FATEFUL DELAY

Melas was confident that the French were beaten. Having been wounded slightly earlier in the action, he turned command over to Major-General Anton Zach, his chief of staff, with instructions to carry on chasing the battered foe. Zach, however, delayed resuming the pursuit, and instead allowed his men a short break to go foraging for food. The delay gave Napoleon – by this time reinforced by the returning division – the chance to reorganize his troops.

When Zach finally attacked, he and his men advanced in column to launch a head-on assault. His intention was to break up the French before they could reform completely. The attack did not go well. As Zach's column approached, the French massed all their remaining artillery together and opened fire. The initial assault was repelled by Napoleon's fresh infantry, which then launched a devastating

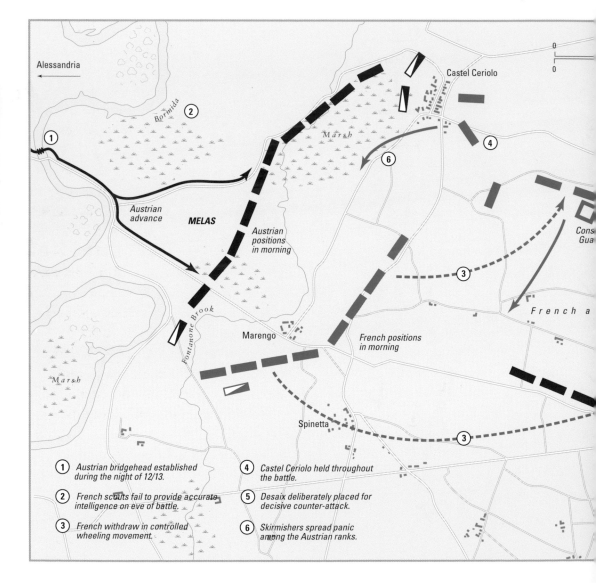

Alessandria

Bormida

Castel Ceriolo

Marsh

Austrian advance

MELAS

Austrian positions in morning

Fontanone Brook

French positions in morning

Marengo

Marsh

Spinetta

Cons Gua

French a

1. Austrian bridgehead established during the night of 12/13.

2. French scouts fail to provide accurate intelligence on eve of battle.

3. French withdraw in controlled wheeling movement.

4. Castel Ceriolo held throughout the battle.

5. Desaix deliberately placed for decisive counter-attack.

6. Skirmishers spread panic among the Austrian ranks.

counter-attack. They hurled themselves at the Austrian column, shattering its leading brigade. Zach countered by ordering General Franz Lattermann's grenadiers forward to resume the attack.

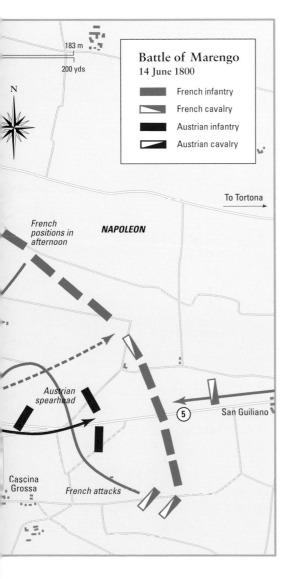

French positions in afternoon

NAPOLEON

To Tortona

183 m

200 yds

N

Battle of Marengo
14 June 1800

French infantry

French cavalry

Austrian infantry

Austrian cavalry

Austrian spearhead

⑤ San Guiliano

Cascina Grossa

French attacks

This was the turning point of the battle as Napoleon seized his opportunity. Sending his infantry forwards again, he ordered General Kellermann's heavy cavalry to charge headlong into the grenadiers' left flank. The Austrians at the front of the column promptly threw down their arms and surrendered; Zach himself was captured in the debacle.

Panic spread through the Austrian ranks as Kellermann's cavalry went on to rout the dragoons who were supposed to be supporting Lattermann's brigade. The fleeing dragoons crashed into the main body of the Austrian infantry, scattering it to the four winds. In the ensuing chaos, the Austrian rearguard mounted a last-ditch stand around Marengo. This allowed the rest of the army to recross the Bormida and reach the safety of Alessandria.

The next day, Melas began negotiating for peace terms. The result was the Convention of Alessandria, by which the Austrian agreed to evacuate all of north-western Italy west of the river Ticino and to suspend operations throughout the rest of the country. Napoleon had turned what looked like certain defeat into another triumph for French arms.

The map shows the movements made by the French and British armies during the Battle of Marengo.

Trafalgar

NELSON'S VICTORY OVER THE COMBINED FRENCH AND SPANISH FLEETS AT TRAFALGAR IN 1805 PUT AN END TO NAPOLEON'S HOPES OF DEFEATING BRITISH NAVAL POWER. IT SET THE SEAL ON BRITAIN'S ENDURING NAVAL SUPREMACY.

Although frequently regarded as the crucial battle that frustrated Napoleon's invasion of Britain, Trafalgar was fought a month after the emperor had actually abandoned the plan. He and the Grande Armée were campaigning on the river Danube in late October 1805, when Nelson and Admiral Pierre de Villeneuve clashed in one of the decisive encounters of naval history.

Earlier that year, however, de Villeneuve's activities had been closely linked to the threatened invasion. Bottled up in Toulon by the British, he had broken through the blockade to meet Admiral Federico Gravina's Spanish squadron from Cadiz. The combined Franco-Spanish fleet then lured Nelson across the Atlantic, all the way to the Caribbean, before doubling back to reach European waters once again.

De Villeneuve reluctantly set sail for the Straits of Gibraltar, little knowing that, just over the horizon, Nelson was lying in wait.

Napoleon expected de Villeneuve, having escaped Nelson, to make for Brest to join with the blockaded French squadrons then. The reinforced fleet would then sweep down the English Channel and convoy the French invasion barges across it from Boulogne. De Villeneuve was not keen on the plan. Discovering that the Royal Navy was again on his trail, he exploited a loophole in his orders to make for Spain, sailing first to Ferrol and then on to Cadiz. On the way, he clashed with Admiral Robert Calder at Cape Finisterre, but managed to fight his way clear.

De Villeneuve was not left in peace for long. Napoleon soon hounded him out to sea again – this time, ordering him into the Mediterranean to support a French attack on Naples. De Villeneuve, however,

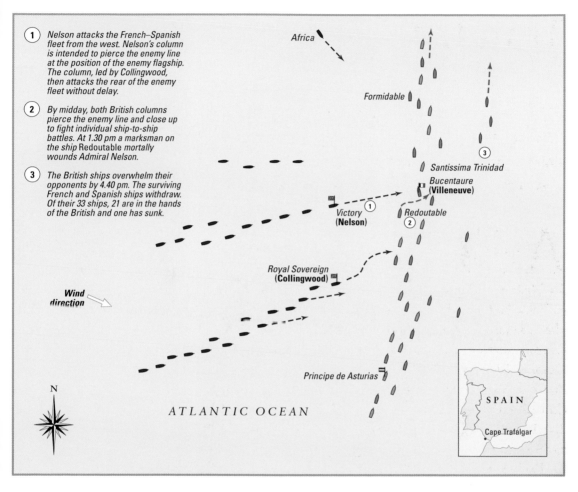

1. Nelson attacks the French–Spanish fleet from the west. Nelson's column is intended to pierce the enemy line at the position of the enemy flagship. The column, led by Collingwood, then attacks the rear of the enemy fleet without delay.

2. By midday, both British columns pierce the enemy line and close up to fight individual ship-to-ship battles. At 1.30 pm a marksman on the ship Redoutable mortally wounds Admiral Nelson.

3. The British ships overwhelm their opponents by 4.40 pm. The surviving French and Spanish ships withdraw. Of their 33 ships, 21 are in the hands of the British and one has sunk.

Africa

Formidable

Santissima Trinidad

Bucentaure
(Villeneuve)

Victory
(Nelson)

Redoutable

Royal Sovereign
(Collingwood)

Wind direction

Principe de Asturias

N

ATLANTIC OCEAN

SPAIN

Cape Trafalgar

was reluctant to obey. The infuriated emperor, finally losing patience with his admiral's continued procrastination, threatened to replace him if he did not obey. As a result, on 19 October 1805, de Villeneuve reluctantly set sail for the Straits of Gibraltar, little knowing that, just over the horizon, Lord Nelson and his fleet were lying in wait.

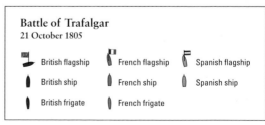

Battle of Trafalgar
21 October 1805

British flagship   French flagship   Spanish flagship

British ship   French ship   Spanish ship

British frigate   French frigate

The map shows the movements made by the French, Spanish and British fleets at the Battle of Trafalgar.

THE FLEETS CLASH

Nelson's battle plan was unorthodox. He decided that his fleet should close in on the enemy in two lines ahead, the aim being to pierce the Franco-Spanish battle line in two places – in the centre and towards the rear – and then to force a ship-to-ship engagement. Confident that superior British ship handling and naval gunnery would win him the day, he told his assembled captains that his aim was to annihilate the whole Franco-Spanish fleet.

Shortly after dawn on 21 October, the fleets sighted one another. Carrying

out Nelson's plan, the windward British column closed up around his flagship, the *Victory*, while the leeward column formed up behind the *Royal Sovereign*, which was flying Admiral Cuthbert Collingwood's flag. Villeneuve immediately ordered his fleet to reverse its course and make a run for it back to Cadiz. The move put him on a collision course with Nelson's ships, which were making their final preparations for the fight.

'ENGLAND EXPECTS'

The battle began shortly after midday. Collingwood's ships engaged the rear of the Franco-Spanish fleet, piercing its line as intended, and then breaking off to fight ship-to-ship duels. Nelson's ships, too, were quickly in action. Soon, Villeneuve's van had been separated from the rest of his fleet, while vessel after vessel in his centre and rear found themselves being pounded mercilessly by broadside after broadside.

Nelson was on the brink of total victory, but he did not survive to enjoy its glory. At around 1.15 pm, while the *Victory* was locked in a ferocious ship-to-ship duel with the *Redoubtable*, a French marksman caught sight of the British admiral in his vice-admiral's uniform, wearing all his medals and decorations. The sniper took careful aim and shot Nelson down with a single bullet that penetrated his shoulder, one of his lungs and pierced his spine.

Nelson was hurried down to the surgeons below deck. Though mortally wounded, he survived for three hours while the battle reached its climax. The *Redoubtable* came under fire from both sides as the *Temeraire* joined in the fight. Eventually its exhausted crew gave up the unequal struggle. The monster *Santissima Trinidad*, the flagship of Spanish rear admiral Baltazar de Cisneros, was also out of the fight. By the time Nelson died at 4.30 pm, 18 French and Spanish ships had struck their colours; 17 were in British hands and one was a blazing wreck. Villeneuve himself had been forced to surrender the *Bucentaure*, his crippled flagship, to the aptly named *Conqueror* and was now a prisoner. The British had not lost a single vessel.

Collingwood assumed command of the fleet and its battered prizes. As he was convoying them towards Gibraltar, a massive storm blew up, which forced him to abandon all but four of his prizes. Only 11 French and Spanish ships managed to disengage and limp back to Cadiz. The triumph was complete, but Britain had lost her most gifted naval commander with the death of Lord Nelson.

HMS Victory, *Nelson's flagship at the Battle of Trafalgar; now in dry dock at Portsmouth, where she serves as a museum.*

Austerlitz

WIDELY REGARDED AS NAPOLEON'S TACTICAL MASTERPIECE, THIS DECISIVE ENCOUNTER SAW HIM DEFEAT THE COMBINED ARMIES OF AUSTRIA AND RUSSIA. IT IS OFTEN REFERRED TO AS THE 'BATTLE OF THE THREE EMPERORS'.

The campaign that reached its climax at Austerlitz in December 1805 began in early autumn. As the Austrian army, commanded by General Karl Mack, marched into Bavaria, Napoleon responded by abandoning his planned invasion of Britain. Instead, he led his Grande Armée across the Rhine to confront the Austrians. Napoleon's plan was to tie down Mack and his forces while the bulk of his army executed a dramatic wheel through Franconia and northern Bavaria, aiming to reach the Danube, sever Mack's line of retreat and then attack his army from the rear.

The daring manoeuvre was a complete success. Cut off and surrounded at Ulm, Mack capitulated on 25 October. Napoleon immediately advanced on Vienna, which he occupied early the following month.

On the face of it, Napoleon's position looked formidable, but in reality he faced a major new threat. The Russians were arriving on the scene. Through skilful manoeuvring, General Mikhail Kutuzov, their wily commander, avoided being trapped south of the Danube. He retreated northwards towards Olmutz to link up with the remains of the Austrian army and a second Russian force led by General Buxhowden. Between them, the Russians and Austrians now had 85,000 troops in the field. By contrast, the French emperor had only around 53,000 men under his immediate command by the time he reached Brno in late November.

Napoleon was faced with a dilemma. Common sense counselled that it was too

> *Napoleon was faced with a dilemma. Common sense counselled that it was too risky to force battle in the face of unfavourable odds.*

Phases 1 and 2 of the Battle of Austerlitz, illustrating the movements made by Napoleon and Alexander I.

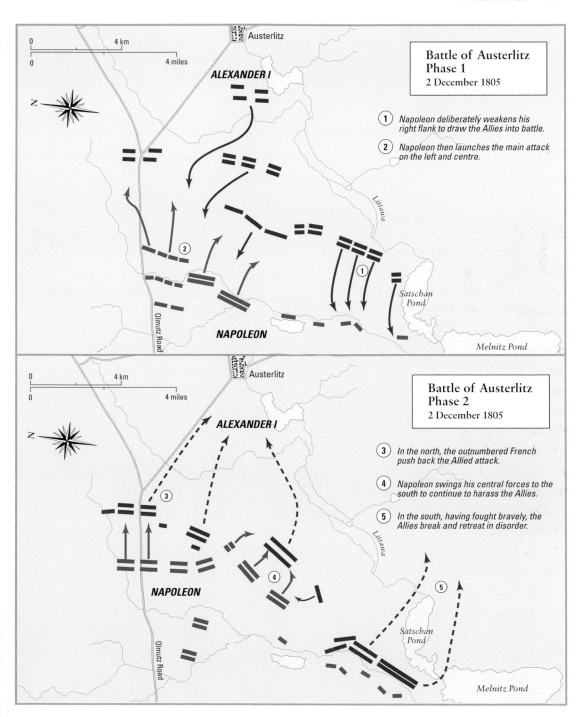

**Battle of Austerlitz
Phase 1**
2 December 1805

1 *Napoleon deliberately weakens his right flank to draw the Allies into battle.*

2 *Napoleon then launches the main attack on the left and centre.*

**Battle of Austerlitz
Phase 2**
2 December 1805

3 *In the north, the outnumbered French push back the Allied attack.*

4 *Napoleon swings his central forces to the south to continue to harass the Allies.*

5 *In the south, having fought bravely, the Allies break and retreat in disorder.*

risky to force battle in the face of such unfavourable odds. Even a minor reverse might well turn into a major disaster, especially since it looked more than likely that Prussia was on the brink of entering the war against him. On the other hand, it was vital for him to win a decisive victory before his position in Moravia became untenable. He resolved to fight. The battle would take place on the grounds of his choosing, around the Pratzen Heights near the small town of Austerlitz.

An engraving of the emperor Napoleon, who won a decisive and brilliant victory at the Battle of Austerlitz.

SETTING A TRAP

At his best when facing a crisis, Napoleon set about turning his apparent weakness to his advantage. His first move was to convince his foes that he wished to avoid a clash – in a parley, he indicated to Count Dolgoruki, Tsar Alexander I's aide de camp, that he was willing to negotiate rather than face attack. Then he feigned a panicked withdrawal from the Pratzen Heights. On 1 December, the Russian and Austrian troops were allowed to occupy them unopposed.

What Napoleon was waiting for were the reinforcements he had summoned. Bernadotte's I Corps was the first to arrive, followed by Davout's III Corps, the advance guard of which had marched day and night to cover the distance of 96 km (60 miles) from Vienna in less than 72 hours. Napoleon's plan was for General Claude Legrand to hold his right wing, while Davout's corps made a concealed approach to support him from the south. The bulk of the army was concentrated on the left, where Lannes' V Corps occupied a feature called the Santon, with Bernadotte's corps concealed behind it. In the centre were Soult's IV Corps, Oudinot's grenadiers, while Murat's cavalry was stationed around Zurlan Hill.

Napoleon's hope was that Kutuzov and the other allied commanders would attack his right wing with the bulk of their forces. That was exactly what they decided to do. Their plan was for Buxhowden to strike at Napoleon's right with 45,000 men; a further 13,000, commanded by Prince Bagration, would attack the Santon positions. The Russians and Austrians were falling neatly into the trap that Napoleon had set for them. Not only would they find that the French right was stronger than they anticipated; by stripping their centre of troops they were leaving themselves wide open to devastating attack.

BATTLE IN THE MIST

Dawn on 2 December was cold, with dense mist cloaking the battlefield. The Russians started their march to get into position at 4.00 am and eventually attacked two hours later. Buxhowden, however, met with far stiffer resistance than he had expected and responded by summoning reinforcements. The French were also holding their own against Bagration. Then, at 9.00 am, as the sun broke through the mist, Napoleon ordered Soult to seize the Heights.

Kutuzov finally realized how completely he had been deceived. Desperately, he tried to recall troops from his left, but by midday the French were firmly in possession of the heights, repulsing all his attempts at counter-attack. Eventually, the allied forces fell back in wholesale retreat. The next day, as the Russians marched hard for Poland, Francis I, the Austrian emperor, met Napoleon and sued for peace. The French emperor had won his greatest victory.

FACT FILE

Austerlitz

Date: 2 December 1805

Location: Near Austerlitz, Moravia; Czech Republic

Historical Context: War of the Third Coalition (1803–1806)

States Involved: French Empire; Russian Empire; Austrian Empire

Commanders and Leaders: Napoleon I, Soult (France); Francis II (Austria); Alexander I, Mikhail Kutuzov, Prince Bagration (Russia)

Outcome: Decisive French victory

Aftermath: One of Napoleon's greatest victories; marked the end of the Third Coalition

Gettysburg

AN EPIC THREE-DAY BATTLE THAT MARKED THE CLIMAX OF THE SECOND AND FINAL CONFEDERATE ATTEMPT TO INVADE THE NORTH, LEE'S DEFEAT AT GETTYSBURG SIGNALLED THE TURNING OF THE TIDE AGAINST THE CONFEDERACY.

Fought over three days, from 1 to 3 July 1863, Gettysburg was one of the crucial battles of the US Civil War, yet it was an engagement that both sides stumbled into almost by accident. For almost a month after General Robert E. Lee, the commander of the Army of Northern Virginia, had moved into Pennsylvania from Fredericksburg, facing the Army of the Potomac under Major-General Joseph Hooker, it became clear that both Confederate and Federal intelligence had been faulty. As a result, neither side knew precisely where the other was.

After his plan to advance on Richmond, the Confederate capital, had been turned down by President Abraham Lincoln, Hooker decided to manoeuvre his forces so that they stood between Lee's Confederates and Washington DC, ready to block any advance on the Federal capital. Lee, in the meantime, was marching northwards up the Shenandoah and Cumberland valleys. On 28 June, he got the unwelcome news that, rather than still being in Virginia as he had confidently supposed, the Army of the Potomac was now just 40 km (25 miles) away at Frederick in Maryland. He also learnt that Hooker had been replaced by the far more competent General George G. Meade as the Federal commander.

...it became clear that both the Confederate and Federal armies' intelligence had been faulty. As a result, neither side knew precisely where the other was.

THE FIRST CLASHES

When the battle began, fortune at first favoured the Confederates. In fierce fighting, which led to heavy casualties on both sides, the Federals were forced back

The map shows the positions of the Confederate and Federal units and their artilleries during the Battle of Gettysburg.

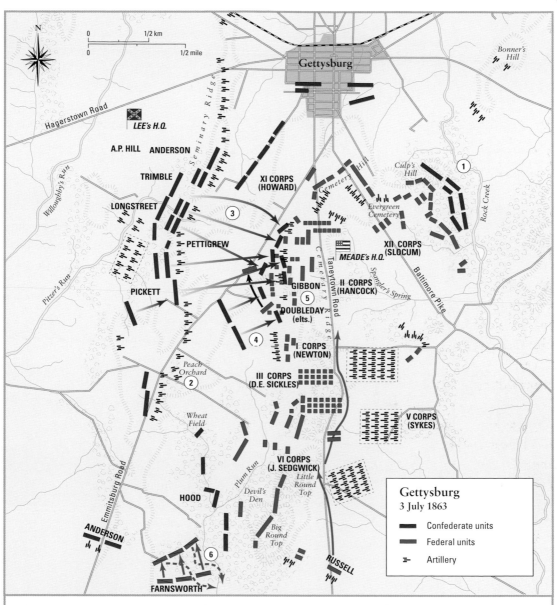

N

0   1/2 km
0   1/2 mile

Bonner's Hill

Gettysburg

Hagerstown Road

LEE's H.Q.

A.P. HILL   ANDERSON

Seminary Ridge

Culp's Hill

TRIMBLE

XI CORPS (HOWARD)

1

Cemetery Hill

LONGSTREET

Evergreen Cemetery

XII CORPS (SLOCUM)

Willoughby's Run

3

PETTIGREW

Rock Creek

MEADE'S H.Q.

II CORPS (HANCOCK)

Pitzer's Run

PICKETT

GIBBON

5

Spangler's Spring

Baltimore Pike

Cemetery Ridge

Taneytown Road

DOUBLEDAY (elts.)

4

I CORPS (NEWTON)

Peach Orchard

2

III CORPS (D.E. SICKLES)

V CORPS (SYKES)

Wheat Field

VI CORPS (J. SEDGWICK)

Little Round Top

Emmitsburg Road

Plum Run

HOOD

Devil's Den

ANDERSON

Big Round Top

RUSSELL

6

FARNSWORTH

Gettysburg
3 July 1863

▬▬ Confederate units

▬▬ Federal units

⊥⊥ Artillery

1. 3 July, 5.30 am–10.00 am: *Johnson's division of Ewell's corps launches repeated atttacks on Culp's Hill but makes no progress.*

2. 1.00 pm: *Confederate artillery cannonade begins with 140 cannons, the Federals reply with 80 guns.*

3. 3.00 pm: *Pickett's, Pettigrew's and Trimble's Confederate infantry attack towards Seminary Ridge.*

4. 3.30 pm: *Stannard's Federal brigade attacks flank of Pickett's division.*

5. 3.45 pm: *Limit of Confederate infantry attacks.*

6. 5.30 pm: *Farnsworth's cavalry charge against Confederate right is beaten off with heavy losses.*

through the town. They regrouped to the south along the high ground near the cemetery. Lee, who arrived on the scene late that afternoon, ordered General Richard S. Ewell, commander of his 2nd Corps, to take the ground, but unfortunately added the words 'if practical' to the order. The over-cautious Ewell confined himself to probing the Federal positions.

By the time Lee realized Ewell had not attacked, the opportunity had vanished. The Federals, now reinforced, had been

By the time Lee realized Ewell had not attacked, the opportunity had vanished. The Federals, now reinforced, had been given time to dig in.

given time to dig in. They consolidated their hold on Cemetery Hill, Culp's Hill and along Cemetery Ridge itself, anchoring their left flank on two more hills – Little Round Top and Big Round Top. General James Longstreet, in command of Lee's 1st Corps, considered the position to be almost impregnable. He counselled Lee not to attack it, suggesting that the army

An engraving of the Gettysburg battlefield, Pennsylvania, scene of one of the decisive turning points in the Civil War.

should move to the east, get between the Army of the Potomac and Washington and take up its own defensive position, forcing the Federals to attack it instead. Lee turned down Longstreet's advice.

THE DECISIVE DAY

The next morning, Lee ordered Longstreet to attack the Federal left wing and Ewell to assault Cemetery Hill and Culp's Hill. Longstreet met with mixed fortunes. Though he drove the Federal troops back from the Peach Orchard, Wheatfield and Devil's Den, he failed to break through their main line. It may have been that, thanks to delaying his attack, he missed the chance to do so.

Before the attack began, General Daniel Sickles, the 3rd Corps' commander, unilaterally decided to move his troops off Little Round Top. If the Confederates had managed to take it, they would have been able to enfilade the entire Federal position. Fortunately for the Federal Army, Major-General Gouverneur K. Warren, the army's chief engineer, recognized the danger and rushed fresh infantry and artillery to the hill's summit. They got there just in time to repel the Confederates.

Ewell's attack was also unsuccessful. He failed to take either of the positions he assaulted, though he did manage to gain some ground.

PICKETT'S CHARGE

Lee believed that the Federals were nearly beaten and it would take just one last push to bring about their collapse. The next day, he ordered General George Pickett, in command of 15,000 fresh troops, to launch an all-out assault on the Federal centre, while Ewell resumed his attack on the Culp's Hill position. Things, however, did not go according to plan. A Federal counter-attack drove Ewell's troops back from the ground they had won. Everything now rested on Pickett.

After a protracted bombardment from his artillery, Picket led the cream of the Confederacy forwards. They had 1.5 km (1 mile) of open ground to cross before they reached the Federal positions. Almost from the start, they were shelled heavily by the Federal artillery. Then, as they neared the ridge, the Federal infantry joined in the battle. Cut down by cannon and musketry fire, only some 150 Confederate soldiers managed to reach the Federal lines. These meagre few were promptly overwhelmed by superior numbers.

As the survivors drifted back towards their own lines, Lee rode out to meet them. 'It is all my fault', he told them. The next night, the Army of Northern Virginia began its long retreat. The tide of war had turned permanently against the Confederacy.

Vicksburg

GENERAL ULYSSES S. GRANT'S SUCCESSFUL SIEGE OF VICKSBURG IN 1863 WAS AN IMPORTANT TURNING POINT IN THE CIVIL WAR. WITH THE LOSS OF THIS STRONGHOLD ON THE MISSISSIPPI, THE CONFEDERACY WAS CUT IN HALF.

Grant's campaign to capture Vicksburg and so secure control of the Mississippi River for the Union began in winter 1862, but initially the Federal commander met with nothing but setbacks. The so-called 'Gibraltar of the West' proved a tough nut to crack.

That summer, Vicksburg had come under attack for the first time when Admiral David G. Farragut sailed his Federal fleet up the Mississippi from New Orleans and bombarded the city heavily. Jefferson Davis, the President of the Confederacy, reacted immediately. He told Lieutenant-General John C. Pemberton that the city had to be held at all costs. President Lincoln was equally quick to recognize the city's strategic importance. 'Vicksburg is the key', he said. 'The war can never be brought to an end until the key is in our pocket.' Lincoln decided that the taciturn, whisky-drinking Grant was the general who stood the best chance of securing him the key.

Many powerful politicians...were calling for Grant's head. Lincoln, however, still had faith in him. 'I can't spare this man, he fights,' he said. 'I'll try him a little longer.'

GRANT MOVES SOUTH

Grant's campaign, which began in December, got off to an inauspicious start. He started by dividing his army into two. One column, under his personal command, marched overland from Grand Junction, Tennessee, into northern Mississippi; the other, led by Major-General William T. Sherman, pushed down the river itself. The plan was to take the city in a two-pronged attack.

Moving southwards along the railway, Grant was forced to turn back to Memphis, when a series of Confederate cavalry raids on his ever-lengthening lines of communication culminated in the capture of Holly Springs, his main supply depot. Sherman was not having any better luck. The Confederates drove him back when he attempted to strike just north-east of Vicksburg along the banks of the Chickasaw Bayou. He tersely reported to Grant: 'I reached Vicksburg at the time appointed, landed, assaulted and failed.'

Further attempts to bypass Vicksburg's defences and attack the city from the rear were also unsuccessful. By March 1863, newspapers throughout the North and many powerful politicians in Washington were calling for Grant's head. Lincoln, however, still had faith in him. 'I can't spare this man, he fights. I'll try him a little longer', he said.

A NEW PLAN OF ATTACK

Meanwhile, Grant had concluded his best course of action was to advance to the western bank of the Mississippi, search for a favourable crossing point and then strike at Vicksburg from the south and east. Everything, however, depended on whether the Federal fleet, now commanded by Rear-Admiral David Dixon Porter, could manage to run the gauntlet of Vicksburg's massed artillery. Porter waited for a dark, moonless night to make his move. On 16 April, his ships broke through, losing only one transport in the process. Linking up with Grant at Bruinsberg, they began ferrying his men across the river.

Once ashore, Grant pushed his troops rapidly inland. They defeated the Confederates at Fort Gibson before turning north-east to cut the vital rail link between Jackson and Vicksburg itself. The Confederates resisted him stoutly at Raymond, Jackson, Champion's Hill and Big Black River, but, overwhelmed by sheer weight of numbers, they were forced to fall back and back.

STARVED INTO SURRENDER

On 17 May, the routed remnants of Pemberton's army started pouring into Vicksburg; the next day, Grant and his men reached the outskirts of the city. Anxious for a speedy victory, the Federal commander ordered an immediate attack. On the morning of 19 May, after a massive artillery bombardment of the Confederate lines, his troops moved forwards.

Pemberton managed to repel the assault. The same thing happened three days later. Grant decided that there was no alternative to a siege.

Over the next weeks, the Federals extended their lines to the right and the left until they had encircled the entire city. Pemberton was now cut off from any prospect of relief. While his men and Vicksburg's citizens began to starve – by the end of the month, they were reduced to eating cats, dogs and even rats – Grant sapped his way forwards nearer and nearer to the Confederate defences. Eventually, he was close enough for his engineers to lay huge mines under two key forts.

The first mine was detonated on 25 June, but the infantry assault that followed failed. The second followed on 2 July. Meanwhile, Pemberton had decided that the time had come to put an end to the fighting and to the siege. The next day, he requested a parley and asked the Federal commander what terms he would offer him

if he surrendered. On 4 July, white flags were raised above the fortifications and the surviving Confederates marched out to lay down their arms. After a siege lasting 47 days, Vicksburg had capitulated at last and was securely in the hands of the Union.

The map shows the movements made by the Confederate and Federal forces during the Battle of Vicksburg.

FACT FILE
Vicksburg

Dates: 1862–1863

Location: Vicksburg, Mississippi

Historical Context: American Civil War (1861–1865)

States Involved: Union; Confederacy

Commanders and Leaders: General Ulysses S. Grant, Major-General William T. Sherman (Union); Lieutenant-General John C. Pemberton (Confederacy)

Outcome: Decisive Union victory

Aftermath: A turning point in the Civil War; effectively split the Confederacy in half

(1) Autumn/Winter 1862–1863: *Confederates build 14 km (9 miles) of earthworks guarding land approaches to Vicksburg.*

(2) 17 May 1863: *Pemberton and two Confederate divisions retreat into Vicksburg perimeter.*

(3) 17–19 May: *Grant's army approaches Vicksburg. Sherman goes via Benton and Graveyard roads, McPherson via Jackson Road and McClernand via Baldwin's Ferry Road.*

(4) 18 May: *Confederates occupy and strengthen Vicksburg perimeter.*

(5) 19 May: *Grant assails Confederate works but is repulsed.*

(6) 20–22 May, dawn: *Grant emplaces artillery and occupies ground closer to Confederate perimeter.*

(7) 22 May, 6.10 am: *Union artillery and Porter's ironclads moving upriver, bombard Vicksburg.*

(8) 22 May: *Grant assails Confederate defences from 26th Louisiana Redoubt to Square Fort. Porter attacks South Fort. Union troops repulsed with heavy losses.*

(9) 25 May: *As Confederate defences prove too strong to storm, Grant calls for siege operations and reinforcements.*

(10) 27 May: *USS Cincinnati, moving downriver, is sunk while attempting to gauge the strength of Confederate upper water batteries.*

(11) 25 May–3 July: *Union troops forge an iron ring around the defences within the perimeter of Vicksburg.*

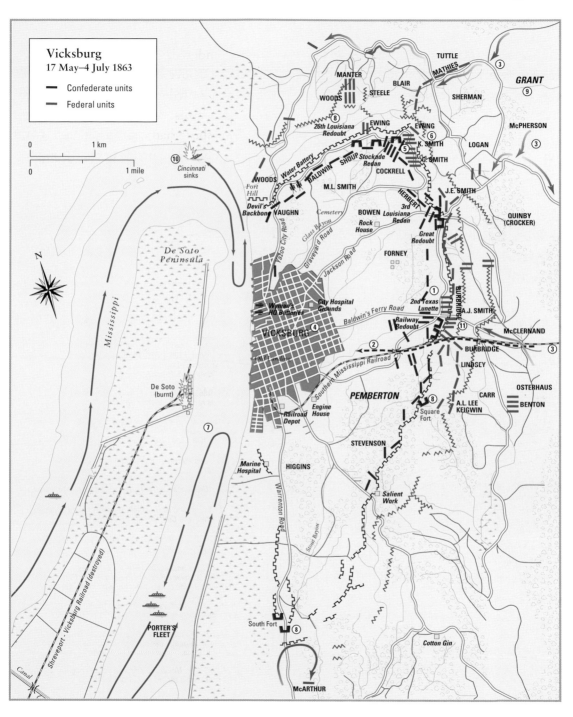

Vicksburg
17 May–4 July 1863

▬▬ Confederate units

▬▬ Federal units

0 ————— 1 km

0 ————— 1 mile

N

TUTTLE
MATHIES
MANTER
BLAIR
WOODS
STEELE
SHERMAN
GRANT ⑨
③
EWING
EWING
26th Louisiana Redoubt ⑧
⑥
K. SMITH
⑤
G. SMITH
LOGAN
McPHERSON
③
WOODS
Water Battery
BALDWIN SHOUP
Stockade Redan
COCKRELL
J.E. SMITH
QUINBY (CROCKER)
③
Fort Hill
Devil's Backbone VAUGHN
M.L. SMITH
HERBERT
3rd Louisiana Redan
Cincinnati sinks ⑩
Cemetery
BOWEN
Rock House
Great Redoubt
Glass Bayou
De Soto Peninsula
Yazoo City Road
Graveyard Road
Jackson Road
FORNEY
Mississippi
Wyman's HQ Batteries
City Hospital Grounds
2nd Texas Lunette
BURBRIDGE
A.J. SMITH
VICKSBURG ④
Baldwin's Ferry Road
Railway Redoubt
⑪
McCLERNAND
②
BURBRIDGE
③
Southern Mississippi Railroad
LINDSEY
De Soto (burnt)
PEMBERTON
Engine House
⑧
Square Fort
A.L. LEE KEIGWIN
CARR
OSTERHAUS
BENTON
⑦
Railroad Depot
STEVENSON
Marine Hospital
HIGGINS
Warrenton Road
Salient Work
Stout Bayou
Shreveport - Vicksburg Railroad (destroyed)
PORTER'S FLEET
South Fort ⑧
Cotton Gin
Canal
McARTHUR

Königgrätz

WHEN THE AUSTRIANS AND PRUSSIANS CLASHED IN BOHEMIA IN JUNE 1866, VICTORY FOR PRUSSIA TRANSFORMED THE EUROPEAN BALANCE OF POWER. SOON, GERMANY WAS UNITED UNDER PRUSSIA'S HEGEMONY.

The battle of Königgrätz – or Sadowa as it is sometimes called – was the turning point in the Seven Weeks' War between Austria and Prussia. In terms of numbers, it was by far the biggest battle fought in Europe during the nineteenth century; between them, the two sides managed to put more than 450,000 men into the field.

The conflict was largely the result of Count Otto von Bismarck's ruthless intrigues. From the moment he became Prussian prime minister in 1862, Bismarck planned to put an end to Austrian influence in Germany. Quarrelling with Austria about which power should control the duchies of Schleswig and Holstein provided him with the pretext he needed to provoke Austria into declaring war. The Austrians were supported by their allies in the German Confederation; Bismarck looked to the newly united Italians, with whom he had recently concluded a secret alliance, for support.

PREPARING FOR ACTION

Count Helmuth von Moltke, Prussia's chief of staff, took command of the Prussian army in the field on 2 June 1866. His opposite number was Field Marshal Ludwig August von Benedek, who had been hand-picked for the job by Franz Josef, the Austrian emperor. In the light of Benedek's previous military exploits, many – including Franz Josef – considered him to be Austria's best general. The only person who did not share this view was Benedek himself. He tried to turn the appointment down, but Franz Josef was adamant that he should accept it.

Moltke began by moving his three armies forwards to take up a position in an arc stretching from Silesia to Saxony. The army of the Elbe concentrated around Halle and Zeitz on the Saxon border; the 1st Army did the same at Torgau and Kottbus and the 2nd Army at Landshut and Reichenbach. Benedek's troops took up position around the fortified town of

Olmutz in Moravia. His intention was to protect Vienna against Prussian attack, but, by choosing to go on the defensive from

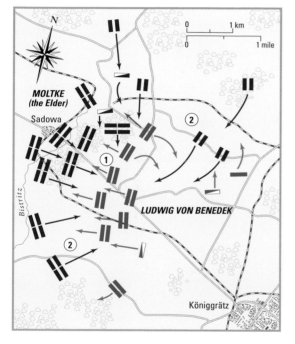

Battle of Königgrätz
1866

- ▬ Prussian infantry
- ▬ Prussian cavalry
- ▬ Railways

- ▬ Austrian infantry
- ▬ Austrian cavalry

(1) Moltke attacks the Austrian army commanded by von Benedek and draws it away from Sadowa.

(2) As the Austrians are engaged in the centre, further Prussian forces arrive and turn the Austrian flanks, enveloping them.

the start, he threw away any chance of gaining the strategic initiative.

Moltke dealt with his German opponents first. On 15 June, General Vogel von Falkenstein forced the Elector of Hanover to capitulate and isolated Bavaria, so forcing two of Austria's most important allies out of the war. The following day, the Army of the Elbe crossed into Saxony. The Saxons withdrew across the river Iser to link up with the Austrian 1st Corps, but, despite Benedek's assurances, no further help was forthcoming. The Prussian advance continued unchecked.

It took Benedek until 30 June to realize that his initial dispositions had been faulty. He immediately telegraphed Franz Josef, urging him to make peace. The emperor had no such intention. Instead, he told Benedek to fight on. The reluctant general had no choice.

THE DECISIVE CLASH

Benedek formed up his army in a rough semicircle on the high ground east of the river Bistritz, its flanks resting on the River

The map shows the movements made by the Prussian and Austrian armies during the Battle of Königgrätz.

Elbe. Moltke responded by planning an ambitious attack. While the Prussian 1st Army demonstrated against the Austrian centre, giving Benedek the impression that it was preparing a mass assault, the 2nd Army would attack the Austrian right flank from the north. The Army of the Elbe would strike at the left.

The battle started around dawn on 3 July when, under the cover of thick mist, the 1st Army began to move forwards. One of its divisions engaged the Austrian outpost at Sadowa, while another crossed the Bistritz and moved south to take the village of Benatek. The Army of the Elbe was slower to get off the mark; however, by 8.00 am, its advance guard had crossed the river and taken Neckanitz. The 2nd Army was substantially delayed.

The next stage of the fighting started at around 8.30 am, when Lieutenant-General Fransecky's 7th Division, which had been ordered forwards to support the Prussians at Sadowa, found itself confronted by the Austrian 2nd and 4th corps, which, without orders, had moved to challenge it.

Around noon, however, Benedek ordered his men back to their original positions. Why he did this is unclear, but it turned out to be a mistaken decision. As the Austrians reluctantly began to retire, the 4th Corps lagging behind the 2nd, the Prussian 2nd Army started to arrive.

The Austrian flank was left exposed to the advancing enemy. The Prussians were quick to take advantage of the unexpected opportunity. By 4.30 pm, with his right flank rapidly falling apart and the Army of the Elbe making headway on the left, Benedek had had enough. He ordered a general retreat. The battle was over. So, too, was the war. Peace was signed in Prague a few days later.

FACT FILE
Königgrätz

Date: 3 July 1866

Location: Sadowa, Bohemia

Historical Context: The Seven Weeks' War (1866)

States Involved: Austria, Saxony; Prussia

Commanders and Leaders: Count Helmuth von Moltke, Prince Friedrich Karl, General Herwarth von Bittenfeld, Crown Prince Friedrich Wilhelm (Prussia); Field Marshal Ludwig August von Benedek (Austria)

Outcome: Decisive Prussian victory

Aftermath: Transformed the European balance of power. Soon, Germany was united under Prussia's hegemony

Otto von Bismarck, Prussian prime minister, was determined to put an end to Austrian influence on Germany.

Sedan

WHEN NAPOLEON III WAS PROVOKED INTO DECLARING WAR ON BISMARCK'S PRUSSIA IN JULY 1870, HE, LIKE MOST OF HIS FELLOW COUNTRYMEN, EXPECTED A QUICK VICTORY. INSTEAD HE MET CATASTROPHIC, SPEEDY AND UTTER DEFEAT.

So great was French confidence in victory when Napoleon III (Napoleon I's nephew and heir) was manoeuvred into declaring war on Prussia in July 1870 that it was generally believed that the conflict would be over within weeks. Few thought that the Army of the Rhine, led by the emperor himself, could be bested on the battlefield. Marshal Edmond Le Boeuf, in charge of France's mobilization, boasted: 'The war with the Prussians will be a mere stroll, stick in hand.' The opposite proved to be true. A string of defeats at Wissembourg, Spicheren and Rezonville forced Marshal Achille Bazaine, who had taken over from Napoleon as the Army of the Rhine's commander, to retreat towards his base at Metz. Defeated again at the battle of Gravelotte on 18 August, he retired into the heavily fortified city, where he was besieged by elements of the Prussian 1st and 2nd armies.

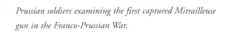

Prussian soldiers examining the first captured Mitrailleuse gun in the Franco-Prussian War.

Marshal Marie de MacMahon, Bazaine's fellow commander, did not fare any better. He was defeated at Worth on 6 August and, like Bazaine, he fell back. He got as far as Chalons-sur-Marne, where his surviving units together with hastily summoned reinforcement were grouped into the Army of Chalons. Napoleon III joined MacMahon, though he did not take over as the army's commander.

Ordered to break through to Bazaine, MacMahon's army started to march north-east towards the Belgian frontier on 21 August. The plan was to turn south towards Metz and fall on the flank of the besieging Prussians. Unfortunately for MacMahon, Field Marshal Helmut von

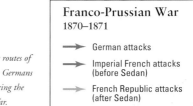

Franco-Prussian War
1870–1871

→ German attacks

→ Imperial French attacks (before Sedan)

→ French Republic attacks (after Sedan)

The map shows the routes of attack taken by the Germans and the French during the Franco-Prussian War.

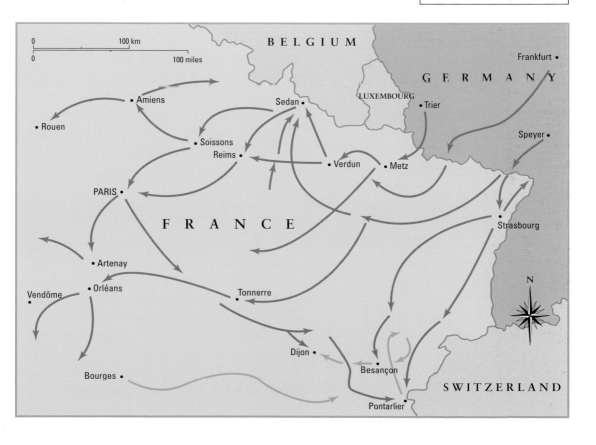

Moltke, the Prussian commander-in-chief, was swift to react. He ordered the Army of the Meuse and his 3rd Army to counter the French advance. After receiving several sharp checks, MacMahon decided his best move was to concentrate his forces around the fortress of Sedan.

Surrounded by high ground and hemmed in by the river Meuse and its tributaries, Sedan was by no means the ideal place to elect to make a stand. Nor was it able to feed MacMahon's army, which began to straggle into a triangle roughly bordered by the Meuse and two other rivers on 30 August. There was less than two days' supply of food in the town.

Moltke realized this was his opportunity to deal the French, many of whom were already demoralized, a crippling blow. The Army of the Meuse was to block any attempt by the French to escape to the east, while the 3rd Army was to press against the front and right flank of MacMahon's troops. By falling back on Sedan, the French commander actually made it easier for Moltke to implement his plan.

Heir and nephew of the emperor Napoleon, Napoleon III was manipulated into declaring war on Prussia in 1870.

THREE COMMANDERS IN TWO HOURS

The battle began early on 1 September, when a detachment of the 1st Bavarian Corps found the railway bridge south of Bazeilles was still intact. They crossed it, only to be driven back by a French counter-attack. Before the bridge could be blown up, however, the Bavarians attacked again, advancing as far as Bazeilles under cover of a thick fog. The French drove the Bavarians back again.

MacMahon, who had come to see what was going on, was wounded by a shell splinter. He delegated his responsibilities to General Alexandre Ducrot, commander of the 1st Corps, who decided to withdraw from Sedan to a better fighting position to the north. Then fate took a hand. General Emmanuel-Felix de Wimpffen, who had arrived from Paris the previous day, produced a letter from the war minister ordering him to take over from MacMahon should the latter be incapacitated. He promptly countermanded Ducrot's orders.

Moltke realized this was his opportunity to deal the French, many of whom were already demoralized, a crippling blow.

Wimpffen believed that he could capitalize on the success of the French counter-attack, drive the Prussians into the Meuse and win a great victory. He was mistaken. While French eyes were fixed on the battle raging around Bazeilles, troops from Moltke's 3rd Army had crossed the Meuse and were already starting to push north. By noon, the French army was encircled.

After desperate cavalry charges to open an escape route failed, Napoleon III decided to intervene. Realizing the futility of further resistance, he ordered the white flag to be raised. Wimpffen countermanded the emperor and ordered a last-ditch attempt to be made to break out to the south. It failed as well. Napoleon rode out to ask the Prussians for a truce. The next day, he met Bismarck on the road to Moltke's headquarters and officially capitulated. News of the surrender led to revolution in Paris, the fall of the dynasty and the proclamation of the Third Republic. Though the war dragged on until May 1871, the defeat at Sedan made its outcome inevitable.

FACT FILE

Sedan

Date: 1 September 1870

Location: The fortress of Sedan on the river Meuse

Context: The Franco-Prussian War (1870–1871)

States Involved: France; Prussia

Commanders and Leaders: Napoleon III, General Auguste-Alexandre Ducrot, Marshals Marie de MacMahon, Emmanuel-Felix de Wimpffen (France); Wilhelm I, Ludwig Freiherr von der Tann, Field Marshal Helmut von Moltke (Prussia)

Outcome: Decisive Prussian victory

Aftermath: Led to revolution in Paris, the fall of the dynasty and the proclamation of the Third Republic

Omdurman

WHEN KITCHENER MARCHED ON KHARTOUM AND CRUSHED THE DERVISHES, WHO HAD MURDERED GENERAL GORDON THERE 13 YEARS EARLIER, HE SHOWED THAT FANATICISM WAS NO MATCH FOR MODERN MACHINE GUNS AND ARTILLERY.

Ever since the capture of Khartoum by the Mahdi and his fanatical Dervishes in January 1885, the Sudan had been a boil that British imperialists believed ought to be lanced sooner rather than later. Major-General Sir Herbert Kitchener, appointed Sirdar (commander-in-chief) of the Egyptian army in 1892, was one of them. Sir Evelyn Baring, the imperial proconsul who was ruler of Egypt in all but name, was another. Together, the two men pressurized the British government to sanction a campaign to reconquer the Sudan and avenge the death of General Gordon. In 1896, the government finally gave them the go-ahead.

It was a 1,600 km (1,000 mile) trek south from Cairo to reach the Dervish heartland. Initially, Kitchener convoyed his troops in steamers up the Nile and captured Dongola, a strategically important town just above the river's Third Cataract some 1,029 km (640 miles) north of the Dervish capital. There, he halted. While waiting for further orders, he secured his communications by building a rail link across the desert from Wadi Halfa to terminate at Abu Hamed, at the junction of the River Atbara and the Nile. Eventually, in April 1898, he was given permission to proceed.

Shortly after dawn on 2 September, the battle commenced with what one eyewitness described as an 'awful noise'. It was the sound of the advancing Dervish army.

ON TO OMDURMAN

The first clash between Kitchener's Anglo-Egyptians and the Dervishes took place near Atbara on 8 April 1898. It ended in a Dervish defeat. As Kitchener pushed forwards remorselessly, the main Dervish army moved to block his advance. By 1 September, however, he was nearing his main objectives – the twin cities of Khartoum and Omdurman. The latter was the Dervish capital and so a logical place for their army to make its stand.

After despatching some of his gunboats upriver to shell Omdurman's defences, Kitchener ordered the bulk of his army to bivouac for the night on the banks of the White Nile. His men took up a horseshoe formation with their backs to the river and what in Arabic is called a *zariba* – a tall barricade of thorn bushes – in front of them to protect them against any sudden enemy attack. The troops slept fitfully. Cavalry patrols had reported that some 50,000 Dervishes had taken up station behind a low ridge, only 8 km (5 miles) away from Kitchener's camp.

THE DERVISH ATTACK

Shortly after dawn on 2 September, the battle commenced with what one eyewitness described as an 'awful noise'. It was the sound of the advancing Dervish army. They soon came into sight, as Ronald Meiklejohn, a lieutenant in the Royal Warwickshire Regiment, recorded. 'All along the crests of the high ground to our right', he wrote, 'a solid black multitude of men began to appear. Soon after, another mass appeared over Signal Hill ridge.' The Dervishes, Meiklejohn went on to note, were 'moving forwards

fairly quickly. Then they suddenly slowed down, made a really orderly right wheel, deployed into one huge and nearly uninterrupted line and came straight at us.'

Much to Kitchener's astonishment, the Dervishes were launching an all-out frontal assault on his well-equipped

This Victorian memorial, with allegorical figures representing Fortitude and Faith, is a monument to Gordon of Khartoum in Victoria Embankment Gardens, London. It was unveiled in 1887, two years after his death.

forces, secure in their strong defensive position. As the Dervish line closed in, his artillery started to shell them. Then his infantry opened fire. Their blistering and continuous rifle volleys, supported by rapid machine-gun fire, cut the Dervish ranks to shreds. George Steevens, one of the most celebrated war correspondents of the day, wrote a dramatic account of the resulting carnage. 'They came very fast and very straight', he wrote, 'and presently they came no further. With a crash, the bullets leapt out of the British rifles. It began with the Guards and Warwicks – section volleys at 200 yards – and then, as the Dervishes edged northwards, it ran along to the Highlanders to the Lincolns and to Maxwell's Brigade. The British stood up in double ranks behind their *Zariba*; the Sudanese laid down in their shelter-trench. Both poured out death as fast as they could load and press triggers, shrapnel whistled and Maxims grunted savagely.'

KITCHENER ADVANCES

As the defeated Dervishes started to stream back towards Omdurman, Kitchener ordered the 21st Lancers to harass their retreat. As the cavalry started out, they saw what appeared to be a small band of Dervish cavalry, plus a few foot soldiers, apparently caught in the open. The Lancers wheeled and charged.

It was a trap. Behind the Dervishes the Lancers could see that some 2,000 more lay concealed in a small rocky depression. By the time the Lancers realized they had been duped, it was impossible for them to stop. Fortunately for them, they managed to fight their way out of the depression and rally some 188 meters (200 yards) away. Though the action was short – the young Winston Churchill, who was right in the thick of it, estimated that it lasted no longer than two minutes – it cost them almost a quarter of their strength.

After the event, opinions altered as to whether the charge had been wise. Lieutenant-General Francis Grenfell, commanding British troops in Egypt,

FACT FILE
Omdurman

Date: 2 September 1898

Location: Omdurman

States Involved: Anglo-Egyptians; Mahdist Sudan

Commanders and Leaders: Sir Herbert Kitchener (Anglo-Egyptians); Abdullah al-Taashi (Mahdists)

Outcome: Decisive Anglo-Egyptian victory

The battle of Omdurman, where Anglo-Egyptian forces vanquished the might of the fanatical Dervishes.

wrote that 'despite the very heavy losses in killed and wounded, the action was worthy of the best traditions in British cavalry'. Lieutenant Meiklejohn thought differently. 'We hear that the charge was a great error', he wrote, 'and K is furious.'

There was one more surprise in store for Kitchener. As his infantry started to advance, their right flank and rear were left wide open to a possible Dervish counter-attack. Luckily, Lieutenant-Colonel Hector MacDonald, commander of the Sudanese brigade bringing up the rear, was quick to spot the danger. 'Fighting Mac', as MacDonald was nicknamed, managed to repel an initial Dervish attack and then to manoeuvre his men skilfully to defeat a second Dervish onslaught.

After the battle, Kitchener commented to his staff: 'I think we've given them a good dusting, gentlemen.' Between 10,000 and 11,000 Dervishes had been killed, another 16,000 wounded and 5,000 more taken prisoner. Anglo-Egyptian losses were 28 dead and 145 wounded. General Gordon had been avenged at last.

Total War

In the twentieth century, what became known as total war was the norm on land, sea and in the air. In both world wars, civilians were just as involved as soldiers, sailors and airmen.

Tsushima

WHEN THE JAPANESE NAVY, COMMANDED BY ADMIRAL HEIHACHIRO TOGO, TOOK ON THE RUSSIAN BALTIC FLEET IN THE TSUSHIMA STRAITS IN 1905, THE RESULT WAS ONE OF THE MOST DECISIVE SEA BATTLES IN HISTORY.

When Russia and Japan went to war in 1904, few outside observers expected the Japanese to prevail. By the end of May, General Nogi Maresuke had surrounded Port Arthur, Russia's principal military base in the Far East. In its harbour, the bulk of the Russian Pacific Fleet lay helplessly at anchor. It had been bottled up in the port ever since Admiral Heihachiro Togo had launched a surprise torpedo-boat attack on it in February. As with Pearl Harbor in 1941, the Japanese did not bother with a formal declaration of war.

Tsar Nicholas II ordered his Baltic Fleet to sail for the Far East, break Togo's blockade of the port and re-establish Russian naval supremacy in the Pacific. He put Vice-Admiral Zinovy Rozhestvensky in command of the expedition. Though he lacked combat experience, Rozhestvensky was considered one of Russia's most talented admirals. He was given three months to get the Baltic fleet ready for combat. Then he would have to sail it halfway around the world.

THE NORTH SEA INCIDENT

The voyage did not begin auspiciously. Steaming south through the North Sea, the Russians were thrown into a state of panic when the *Kamchatka*, a fleet repair ship, signalled that it was being attacked by Japanese torpedo boats. Though the *Kamchatka* soon signalled that the mysterious vessels had vanished, the rest of the fleet remained on edge, awaiting the anticipated Japanese attack.

At around midnight, the fleet came across a group of British fishing trawlers. The fishermen fired flares to alert the Russians to their presence. This was enough for Rozhestvensky's nervous crews. Training their searchlights on the trawlers, they promptly opened fire, sinking one trawler and damaging three others. Three fishermen were killed and many more wounded. Already pro-Japanese and outraged by the atrocity, Britain sent the Royal Navy to shadow the Russian fleet. War was only narrowly averted.

Rozhestvensky's difficulties did not end there. The British refused to allow his fleet to sail through the Suez Canal, so it had to take the long passage around the Cape of Good Hope. After a protracted pause at Madagascar, it plodded on, making for Cam Ranh Bay in Indochina, where it was to rendezvous with the Third Pacific Squadron. This was a motley collection of obsolete ships that, despite Rozhestvensky's protests, the government had insisted on despatching to join him. When it arrived in April 1905, it brought him new orders.

After an 11-month siege, Port Arthur had surrendered to the Japanese. Rozhestvensky was ordered to make for Vladivostok, the only Pacific naval base still in Russian hands. Rozhestvensky chose the

Admiral Togo's ships attack the Russian fleet in the battle of Tsushima, with disastrous consequences for the Russian side.

shortest route to his destination – through the Tsushima Straits between the island of Tsushima and the Japanese mainland. Togo anticipated the move, sending out patrols to scout the area. Rozhestvensky tried to slip through the straits by night on 16 May, but was spotted the next morning by the cruiser *Shinano Maru*, which radioed Togo the enemy position. The Japanese admiral immediately put to sea. At around 1.40 pm, the Japanese sighted the Russians

Emperor Meiji ruled during a time of huge social, political and economic change in Japan and witnessed his country's victory in the Russo-Japanese war of 1904–1905, making it a world power.

– still pressing ahead in two long columns. In order to get to windwards of them, Togo altered course, first to the west and then the south-west. Crossing in front of his opponents, he ordered his fleet to follow him as he made a U-turn. It was a risky move, since it had to be executed within range of the Russian guns.

The Russians opened fire; though the *Mikasa*, Togo's flagship, was hit, neither she nor the rest of the Japanese fleet suffered serious damage. Now, steaming parallel to the Russians, the Japanese returned fire. Their superior gunnery soon began to tell. *Suvorov*, Rozhestvensky's flagship, was hit and seriously damaged. The old battleship *Oslyabya* pulled out of line, turned turtle and sank, as did the *Alexander III*, the *Borodino* and the *Suvorov*.

Rozhestvensky did not go down with his ship. Badly wounded earlier in the battle, he was transferred to the destroyer *Buiny*. Rear-Admiral Nicholas Nebogatov took over command of what remained of the battered fleet, which was scattering in confusion. Six cruisers headed for Manila and internment, while one cruiser and two destroyers reached Vladivostok. The six ships with Nebogatov surrendered the next morning. Togo had won one of the greatest victories in naval history.

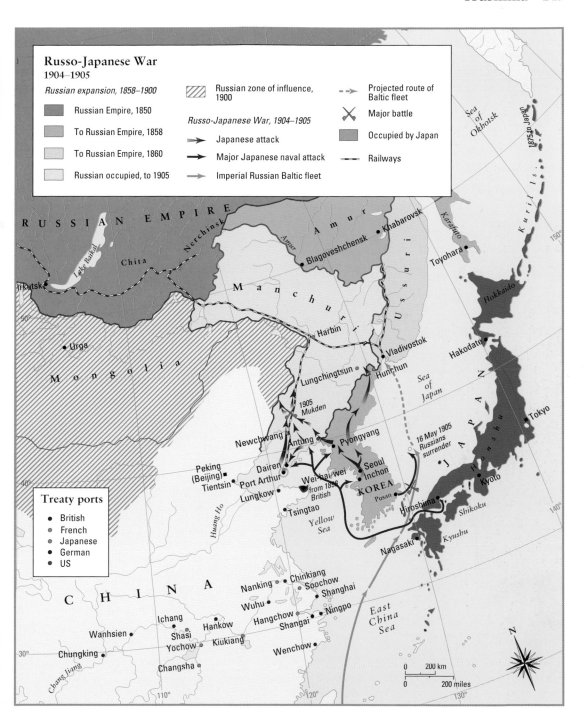

Russo-Japanese War
1904–1905

Russian expansion, 1858–1900

	Russian Empire, 1850
	To Russian Empire, 1858
	To Russian Empire, 1860
	Russian occupied, to 1905

Russian zone of influence, 1900

Russo-Japanese War, 1904–1905

→ Japanese attack

→ Major Japanese naval attack

→ Imperial Russian Baltic fleet

Projected route of Baltic fleet

✕ Major battle

Occupied by Japan

Railways

Treaty ports

- British
- French
- Japanese
- German
- US

Tannenberg

PROBABLY THE MOST SPECTACULAR GERMAN VICTORY OF THE FIRST WORLD WAR, THE BATTLE OF TANNENBERG STOPPED THE RUSSIAN STEAMROLLER IN ITS TRACKS BEFORE IT REALLY GOT STARTED. IT WAS RUSSIA'S WORST DEFEAT OF THE WAR.

Germany's military strategy at the start of the First World War revolved around the Schlieffen Plan. Devised by Count Alfred von Schlieffen, the chief of the German General Staff in 1905, it called for the bulk of the German forces to attack in the west and knock France out of the war. Schlieffen calculated that, in the six weeks he anticipated it would take the slow-moving Russians to mobilize, his armies would crush the French. The troops then could be rushed to the east in ample time to deal with any Russian threat.

As the plan dictated, General Maximilian von Prittwitz and his 8th Army were assigned to defend East Prussia when war broke out. Much to his surprise, Prittwitz found himself confronted by two formidable Russian armies – the 1st under General Pavel Rennenkampf, and the 2nd commanded by General Alexander Samsonov. Responding to French appeals for an immediate offensive to relieve the pressure on the Western Front, the Russians did not wait for their mobilization to be completed before attacking. Instead, they marched into East Prussia, advancing north and south of the Masurian Lakes. Crossing the frontier on 15 August, Rennenkampf moved west, aiming to capture Königsberg and then drive deep into the German heartland. Samsonov reached the border five days later.

> *Rennenkampf did not bother to tell Samsonov what he was doing ... the two Russians disliked each other so much that, at one time, they had actually come to blows.*

THE RUSSIAN STEAMROLLER

On 20 August, General Rennenkampf defeated eight of Prittwitz's divisions at Gumbinnen, while Samsonov's troops were

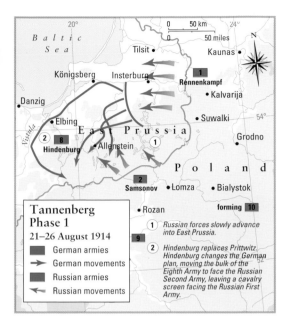

Tannenberg
Phase 1
21–26 August 1914

German armies
German movements
Russian armies
Russian movements

(1) Russian forces slowly advance into East Prussia.

(2) Hindenburg replaces Prittwitz. Hindenburg changes the German plan, moving the bulk of the Eighth Army to face the Russian Second Army, leaving a cavalry screen facing the Russian First Army.

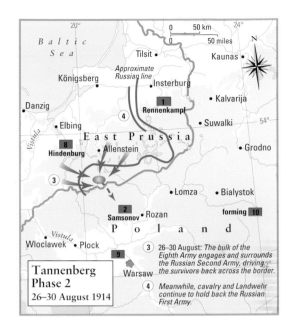

Tannenberg
Phase 2
26–30 August 1914

(3) 26–30 August: The bulk of the Eighth Army engages and surrounds the Russian Second Army, driving the survivors back across the border.

(4) Meanwhile, cavalry and Landwehr continue to hold back the Russian First Army.

starting to lumber into action in the south to threaten the German rear. The German commander lost his nerve. He signalled the high command that he was ordering his army to give up East Prussia and retire behind the line of the river Vistula. The response was immediate. Before Prittwitz could put his orders into effect, he and his deputy were hastily recalled to Berlin. They were replaced by the redoubtable duo of Paul von Hindenburg and Eric von Ludendorff, the latter acting as the former's chief of staff.

When the two men arrived on the Eastern Front on 23 August, it looked as if the Russian offensive might well be crowned by success. Indeed, Helmuth von

Tannenberg
Phase 3
1–14 September 1914

(5) 1–8 September: The Eighth Army re-deploys to face the Russian First Army.

Phases 1, 2 and 3 of the Battle of Tannenberg, illustrating the the movements made by the German and Russian armies.

Moltke the Younger, the overall German commander, had already ordered two army corps to be transferred from the west to prop up the 8th Army if it fell back further. The new commanders, however, were not deterred. Rather than wait for Moltke's reinforcements to reach them, they decided to strike at once.

Colonel Max Hoffman, Prittwitz's deputy chief of staff and chief of operations, had already drawn up a plan for a bold counter-stroke. It called for the bulk of the 8th Army to be concentrated against Samsonov, leaving only a single cavalry division to oppose Rennenkampf, who had temporarily halted his advance. Rennenkampf did not bother to tell Samsonov what he was doing – as the Germans well knew, the two Russians disliked each other so much that, at one time, they had actually come to blows. The Germans also had the advantage of being able to listen into both armies' wireless messages. Incredibly, these were being transmitted in plain language, rather than in code. Hindenburg and Ludendorff endorsed Hoffman's plan.

On 24 August, the over-confident Samsonov, advancing without the benefit of any reconnaissance, blundered into the XX Corps, which was securely entrenched at Orlau-Frankenau. It took him a day to recover from his mauling.

German General Erich von Ludendorff endorsed Hoffman's battle plan.

As he neared Tannenberg, his right wing was attacked by XVII Corps, which forced his troops back. By the evening, the Germans had begun to turn the Russian right. The following day, I Corps broke through the Russian left wing at Usdau and started to work its way around the other flank.

Samsonov was slow to appreciate his peril and, by the time he gave the order to fall back, it was too late. By the evening of 29 August, the Germans had managed to surround the bulk of his troops.

Panic-stricken and disorganized, the Russians were slaughtered as they attempted to break out of the trap. Samsonov, unable to face Tsar Nicholas II with the news of defeat and his disgrace, shot himself the same evening. He left the 2nd Army leaderless and by 31 August, it had ceased to exist.

When he learnt of Samsonov's rout, Rennenkampf, whose greatest fear was of being outflanked in his turn, ordered his army to begin a fighting withdrawal. This culminated in the first battle of the Masurian Lakes, which was fought between 9 and 14 September 1914. Though Rennenkampf extricated himself from an attempted encirclement, he paid a heavy price, losing a colossal 125,000 men and 150 guns in the process. Alexander Samsonov had lost the same number of men and 500 guns at Tannenberg.

FACT FILE

Tannenberg

Date: August–September 1914

Location: Tannenberg, East Prussia

Historical Context: The First World War (1914–1918)

States Involved: Russia; Germany

Commanders and Leaders: Paul von Hindenburg, Erich Ludendorff (Germany); Generals P.K. Rennenkampf, A.V. Samsonov (Russia)

Outcome: Decisive German victory

Aftermath: Stopped the Russians in their tracks before they really got started; Russia's worst defeat of the war

The Marne

WHEN THE FRENCH AND BRITISH MANAGED TO CHECK THE GERMAN ADVANCE ON PARIS ON THE RIVER MARNE IN SEPTEMBER 1914, THE RESULTING BATTLE PUT AN END TO GERMANY'S HOPES OF FIGHTING A QUICK, VICTORIOUS WAR IN THE WEST.

If the Germans had stuck to their original plan when they attacked France in August 1914, the Battle of the Marne might never have been fought. Faced with the likelihood of fighting on two fronts, Count Alfred von Schlieffen, who devised the great battle plan that bore his name, staked everything on winning a quick victory in the west in the event of war. His aim was to force a French surrender in six weeks, before the Russians could complete their mobilization and attack in the east.

What Schlieffen proposed was as follows. The bulk of the French army would be lured into launching an offensive towards the Rhine, while the main German force marched rapidly though neutral Holland, Belgium and Luxembourg to outflank them. The Germans would then execute a huge wheel to the west of Paris, eventually pinning the French army up against the Swiss frontier from the rear. It was a daring scheme, but Schlieffen

believed that it offered his country its best chance of victory. His final words before his death in 1906 – at least reportedly – were 'Only make the right wing strong'.

Luckily for the Allies, Helmuth von Moltke, Schlieffen's irresolute successor, tinkered with the plan. He decided against

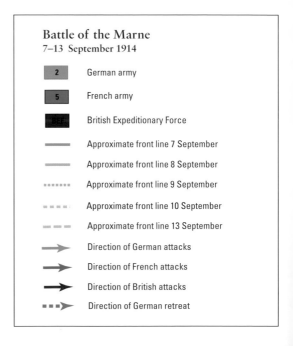

Battle of the Marne
7–13 September 1914

2	German army
5	French army
	British Expeditionary Force
——	Approximate front line 7 September
——	Approximate front line 8 September
········	Approximate front line 9 September
– – –	Approximate front line 10 September
— —	Approximate front line 13 September
→	Direction of German attacks
→	Direction of French attacks
→	Direction of British attacks
■■■▶	Direction of German retreat

Phases 1 and 2 of the Battle of the Marne, illustrating the movements made by the French, British and German armies.

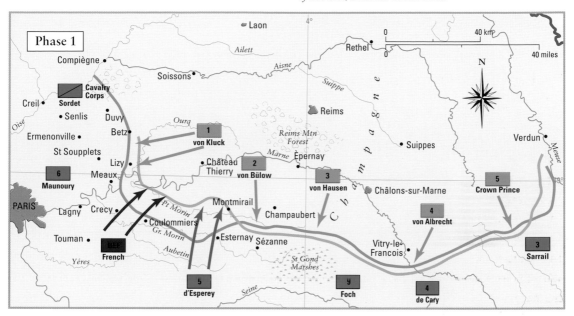

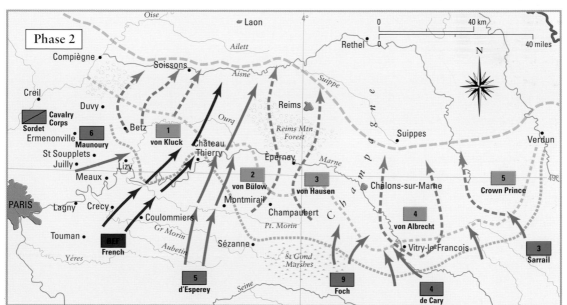

invading Holland. As more troops became available, he strengthened the German left wing, rather than the right. Then, after the outbreak of war, he shifted two army corps from the Western Front to the east in the face of an unexpected Russian offensive. Schlieffen's dream of an irresistible flanking movement was never fulfilled.

THE OPENING MOVES

Nevertheless, German progress was still rapid – particularly that of General Alexander von Kluck's 1st Army. As the French spent their strength in a fruitless offensive in Lorraine, he, together with the 2nd and 3rd armies, swept through Belgium and into northern France. Delaying actions by the Belgians, the BEF (British Expeditionary Force) and the French 5th Army, though heroic, only served to temporarily slow down the German thrust.

> *Thanks to Joffre's prescience, Maunoury was ideally positioned to strike at Kluck's right flank, which was now completely exposed to counter-attack.*

By 30 August, Kluck was nearing Paris. He found himself well ahead of the troops to his left with no apparent enemy threat to his front or on his flanks. Without orders, he shifted his line of advance to the south-east to support the 2nd Army, which was commanded by the more cautious General Karl von Bulow. Together, Kluck reasoned, the two generals would be able to rout what remained of the French 5th Army without difficulty.

JOFFRE STRIKES

It was this final modification of the Schlieffen Plan that was ultimately to prove fatal to German chances of victory. Marshal Joseph Joffre, the French Supreme Commander, quickly divined the Germans' intentions. As the French fell back towards Paris, he boldly rushed units from his right flank to form two new armies.

The 9th Army, commanded by General Ferdinand Foch, was deployed to strengthen the French centre. The 6th Army, under the command of General Michael-Joseph Maunoury, was deployed near the capital.

On 5 September, Maunoury counter-attacked. Thanks to Joffre's prescience, he was ideally positioned to strike at Kluck's right flank, which was now completely exposed to counter-attack. It took Kluck two days to realize his danger. He then quickly fell back north of the river Marne and turned to repel Maunoury. The French were saved by the prompt action of General Gallieni, the Military Governor of Paris, who rushed reserve troops to the front, many of them by taxi, an unorthodox method of transporting military personnel to the front.

Simultaneously with Maunoury's assault, the French 9th and 5th armies had taken the offensive, striking at von Bulow's 2nd Army. The British Expeditionary Force started to advance as well. Though General Sir John French, its commander, had been reluctant to take part in the attack initially, the advance meant that Kluck's left was now under threat as well as his right. As the gap between him and Bulow widened to 40 km (25 miles), the British and French poured through it.

THE 'MIRACLE OF THE MARNE'

At this point, Moltke chose to intervene and on 8 September, he sent Lieutenant-Colonel Richard Hentsch, his Director of Military Intelligence, forwards to find out exactly what was happening. Hentsch first visited Bulow, who was under heavy attack by the 5th Army. He approved the general's decision to retreat. The following day, he ordered the reluctant Kluck to fall back as well. Moltke concurred with this order and ordered a general withdrawal of 64 km (40 miles) back to the north of the river Aisne.

The battle of the Marne was over. Paris had been saved and German intentions in the west had been foiled. The defeat effectively ended all hopes the Germans might have had of bringing the war in the west to a speedy, victorious close. With all prospects of a further advance brought to an end, stalemate and trench warfare were the inevitable results.

FACT FILE
The Marne

Date: 7–13 September 1914

Location: The Marne, France

Historical Context: The First World War (1914–1918)

States Involved: Germany; France; Britain

Commanders and Leaders: General Alexander von Kluck, General Karl von Bulow (Germany); Marshal Joseph Joffre, General Ferdinand Foch, General Michael-Joseph Maunoury (France); General Sir John French (Britain)

Outcome: Decisive Anglo-French victory

Aftermath: Paris was saved; ended all hopes the Germans might have had of winning a speedy victory.

Verdun

THE BATTLE OF VERDUN WAS THE GREATEST AND MOST PROTRACTED BATTLE OF THE FIRST WORLD WAR. THE FRENCH FOUGHT TOOTH AND NAIL TO HOLD OFF THE GERMANS, BUT PAID A TERRIBLE PRICE FOR THEIR EVENTUAL VICTORY.

When General Erich von Falkenhayn, who replaced Moltke as chief of the German general staff after the Marne debacle, decided to attack Verdun, he did not have a big breakthrough in mind. Instead, he opted for a battle of attrition. Falkenhayn calculated that national pride would force the French to defend Verdun regardless of cost.

The German plan was based on their artillery blasting a vast hole through the French defences...then the infantry would advance...

THE GERMANS PREPARE

Since late 1914, the Verdun salient had been relatively peaceful. The French high command was so confident that this would remain the case that it had started to strip some of Verdun's great forts of their guns, reasoning that these could be better employed on more active sectors of the front. This proved to be a regrettable act of supreme folly.

German preparations began on Christmas Eve 1915 in conditions of utmost secrecy. The 5th Army, commanded by the German crown prince himself, was to make the attack and by 1 February, he was almost ready to strike. Over 1,200 guns had been hauled into position on the right bank of the River Meuse. It was an unprecedented concentration of weaponry for an assault front stretching for barely 12 km (8 miles).

The German plan was based on their artillery blasting a vast hole through the French defences. Only then would the infantry advance, from where it had been sheltering in great concrete Stollen, the underground galleries that had been burrowed out throughout the attack zone. As reinforcements moved up to stem the attack, the process would be repeated. In theory, the French would be ground to pieces by the sheer force of the German artillery barrage.

Somewhat belatedly, the French high command rushed troops to the city; these were scheduled to arrive on 12 February, the same day the German crown prince had planned to open his bombardment. Had he been able to do so, catastrophe would have ensued for the French. Fortunately, nature intervened when it began to snow heavily, reducing visibility considerably. With his artillery blinded, the crown prince was forced to postpone the attack until the weather improved. This provided a breathing space.

Preserved First World War trenches at Douaumont near Verdun highlight the grim reality of this form of warfare.

FORT DOUAUMONT FALLS

By 21 February, the weather had cleared. At 7.15 am precisely, the German batteries opened fire and at 4.00 pm, the first German patrols went over the top. The following day, the bulk of the German infantry followed. Though the surviving French defenders put up a heroic resistance, by nightfall virtually the whole of the first French line of defence had fallen into German hands.

There seemed no resisting the relentless German pressure. On 24 February, the whole French second position was taken in a matter of hours. Fort Douaumont, the cornerstone of Verdun's entire defensive system, fell practically without a fight the following day.

General de Castelnau, Joffre's second-in-command, now arrived post-haste from supreme headquarters. His conclusion was stark and simple. Despite the battering the French had taken, the right bank of the Meuse could and would be defended successfully. General Philippe Pétain, whose 2nd Army was already on its way to the city, would take over responsibility for the entire battle.

'THEY SHALL NOT PASS'

Pétain's arrival had an immediate effect. French resistance stiffened as their new commander revitalized the artillery and

The huge cost in lives is made clear by the vast numbers of crosses stretching in countless rows in the Verdun military cemetery.

tackled his supply problems. Supplies poured in and out of the salient along what became known as the Voie Sacrée ('Sacred Way') and fresh troops arrived to reinvigorate the defence.

The Germans concluded that in order to take the city, they needed to attack on the left bank of the Meuse as well as on the right. Like a malignant tumour, the crown prince's offensive had doubled in size. It took the Germans to the end of May to capture Le Mort Homme and Côte 304, the two key hills on the left bank. On 1 June, they attacked on the right bank again. Though cut off and surrounded, Fort Vaux held up the advance for a vital week before surrendering. On 22 June, the

FACT FILE
Verdun

Date: February–December 1916

Location: Verdun, Meuse River

Historical Context: First World War (1914-1918)

States Involved: France, Germany

Commanders and Leaders: General Erich von Falkenhayn, Crown Prince Wilhelm (Germany); Generals Philippe Pétain and Robert Nivelle (France)

Outcome: French victory

Aftermath: Greatest victory of the First World War, but came at a terrible price for the French attack resumed. As the French fell back, General Robert Nivelle, who had taken over from Pétain, issued an impassioned Order of the Day, pledging that 'They shall not pass'.

Then the German thrust faltered. Falkenhayn was forced to rush reserves to the Austrians, who were falling back on the Eastern Front. Haig launched his 'Big Push' on the Somme. On 15 July, the attempt to take the city was abandoned. Falkenhayn was replaced by Hindenburg and Ludendorff. They ordered the crown prince onto the defensive.

Nivelle launched a series of counter-offensives. The crucial moment came in October, when, advancing behind a creeping barrage – Nivelle's inspired tactical innovation – his troops succeeded in recapturing Fort Douaumont and then moved forwards to retake Fort Vaux. By December, they had driven the Germans back almost to their starting point. Verdun had been saved – but at enormous cost.

The map shows the movements made by the Germans and by the French during the Battle of Verdun.

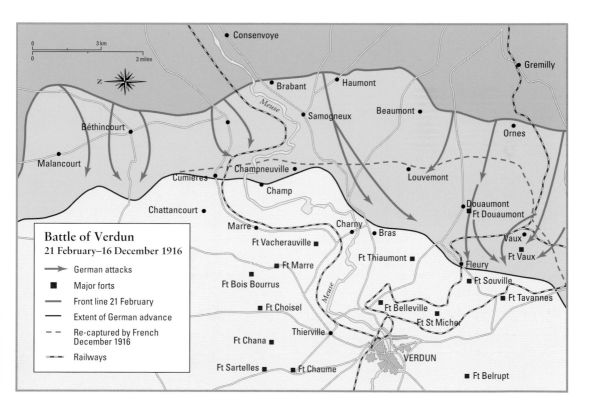

Fall of France

IT TOOK HITLER'S WAR MACHINE JUST SIX WEEKS TO BRING ABOUT THE COLLAPSE OF FRANCE AFTER GERMANY STRUCK IN THE WEST IN MAY 1940. THE LIGHTNING VICTORY THE GERMANS WON WAS AS SUDDEN AS IT WAS UNEXPECTED.

When Hitler's Wehrmacht struck in the West on 10 May 1940, it seemed to many observers that the Schlieffen Plan, with which Germany had gone to war in 1914, was being repeated. Certainly General Maurice Gamelin, the Allied generalissimo, had no doubt this was Hitler's intention. He flung his best-mechanized troops – the British Expeditionary Force (BEF) and the French 7th Army – across the Franco-Belgian border. The BEF was to race to the river Dyle and take up position along its banks, while units of the 7th Army pushed north towards Breda.

SURPRISE IN THE ARDENNES

Had Hitler attacked earlier, this would have been the plan the Wehrmacht would have executed. Unfortunately for Gamelin, the Führer changed his mind. In January 1940, a Luftwaffe aeroplane crash-landed in Belgium with a copy of the attack orders on board. Believing that security had been

fatally compromised, Hitler turned to General Erich von Manstein for advice.

Manstein was something of a maverick who had fallen out of favour with the German high command for criticizing the original plan of attack. Instead, he argued for a bold new redistribution of German forces. Army Group B would still attack first through Holland and Belgium to ensure that Allied attention was focused on that part of the front, but the Schwerpunkt (thrust) of the main attack would be

The map shows the German forces advancing into France, bringing about its collapse in just six weeks.

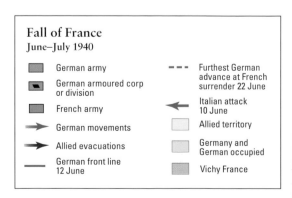

Fall of France
June–July 1940

▭ German army	--- Furthest German advance at French surrender 22 June
▭ German armoured corp or division	← Italian attack 10 June
▭ French army	▭ Allied territory
→ German movements	▭ Germany and German occupied
→ Allied evacuations	
— German front line 12 June	▭ Vichy France

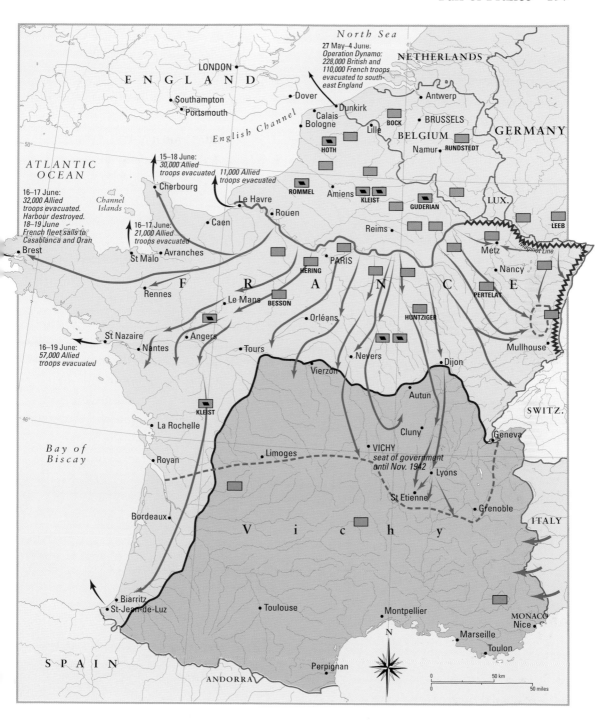

North Sea

27 May–4 June:
Operation Dynamo:
228,000 British and
110,000 French troops
evacuated to south-
east England

NETHERLANDS

LONDON

ENGLAND

Southampton
Portsmouth

Dover

English Channel

Antwerp

BRUSSELS

Calais
Bologne
Dunkirk

BOCK

Lille

BELGIUM

GERMANY

HOTH

Namur

RUNDSTEDT

50°

ATLANTIC
OCEAN

15–18 June:
30,000 Allied
troops evacuated

11,000 Allied
troops evacuated

Cherbourg

ROMMEL

Amiens

KLEIST

GUDERIAN

LUX.

16–17 June:
32,000 Allied
troops evacuated.
Harbour destroyed.
18–19 June:
French fleet sails to
Casablanca and Oran

Channel
Islands

Le Havre

Rouen

Reims

LEEB

Metz

Maginot Line

Brest

16–17 June:
21,000 Allied
troops evacuated

Caen

St Malo
Avranches

HERING

PARIS

Nancy

F R A N C E

PERTELAT

Rennes

Le Mans

BESSON

Orléans

HUNTZIGER

Mullhouse

16–19 June:
57,000 Allied
troops evacuated

St Nazaire

Angers

Tours

Nantes

Nevers

Dijon

SWITZ.

KLEIST

Vierzon

Autun

*Bay of
Biscay*

La Rochelle

Cluny

Geneva

Limoges

VICHY
*seat of government
until Nov. 1942*

Lyons

ITALY

Royan

St Etienne

Grenoble

Bordeaux

V i c h y

Toulouse

Montpellier

Biarritz
St-Jean-de-Luz

MONACO
Nice

Marseille

Toulon

SPAIN

Perpignan

N

ANDORRA

0   50 km
0   50 miles

further to the south through the hilly and heavily forested Ardennes.

The French high command considered the region impassable for tanks. Nevertheless, that was where Manstein proposed concentrating the bulk of Hitler's panzers. Their lightning assault, Manstein assured Hitler, would disorientate the Allies and disrupt all their efforts to launch effective counter-attacks. Hitler ordered the adaptation of the new plan.

> *[Manstein] had fallen out of favour with the German high command for criticizing the original plan of attack...he argued for a bold new redistribution of German forces.*

Everything now went as Manstein had predicted. While the Allies were mesmerized by the German thrust in the north, Army Group A bored its way unnoticed through the Ardennes to emerge near Sedan on the river Meuse on 12 May. In a two-day battle, the panzers forced their way across the river to open up an 80 km (50 mile) gap in the Allied line. Supported

A relic of the Second World War, German panzer divisions played a key role in the attack on France and its subsequent fall in 1940.

by Luftwaffe dive bombers, the panzer divisions powered through the gap as French resistance collapsed.

The question facing the Allies was in which direction the panzers would turn once they had broken out of their bridgeheads. Many believed that they would head straight for Paris, but instead they turned west, sweeping along the Somme Valley to open a corridor to the Channel coast.

THE 'MIRACLE OF DUNKIRK'

Gamelin was sacked on 19 May and General Maxime Weygand replaced him. The situation he faced was desperate in the extreme. The Dutch had capitulated and the Belgians were on the brink of surrender. The British Expeditionary Force and the French 1st Army were surrounded.

The new generalissimo planned a pincer movement to sever the German corridor, the BEF attacking from the north and the French from the south. The British attacked at Arras, but the French did not. Rather than trying to force his way across the corridor to rejoin them, Lord Gort, the BEF commander, decided to fall back to Dunkirk, from where he hoped at least part of the BEF could be extricated.

Had the panzers pressed home their advantage, the evacuation would have been stifled at birth, but they did not.

On 26 May, convinced by Goering's assurance that the Luftwaffe on its own could stop the evacuation, Hitler ordered them to halt. It was not until five days later that German pressure was renewed and by then it was too late. Over the next eight days, 338,226 British and French troops were evacuated successfully from Dunkirk's harbour and its beaches, though they were forced to leave their equipment behind.

THE FINAL ACT

Weygand tried to establish a new defensive position along the Somme, but to little or no avail. The divisions that might have made all the difference were holding the Maginot Line, while France's own armoured divisions had long since been bested by the panzers. Even getting his troops into position proved problematic.

On 5 June, Army Group B swarmed over the Somme, reaching the Seine west of Paris four days later. The next day, Army Group A broke through to the east. The French government fled south, declaring the capital an open city. The Germans marched into Paris on 14 June. What remained of the French army in the field now rapidly disintegrated. On 17 June, Marshal Pétain took over from Paul Reynaud as premier. His first act was to ask Hitler for an armistice. On 22 June, the French surrendered.

Battle of Britain

GOERING BOASTED THAT HIS LUFTWAFFE WAS INVINCIBLE, BUT IN THE SKIES OVER SOUTHERN ENGLAND DURING THE LONG HOT SUMMER OF **1940**, RAF FIGHTER COMMAND'S PILOTS PROVED HIM WRONG. THE 'FEW' BESTED THE MANY.

Following the British refusal to make peace after the fall of France in June 1940, Hitler ordered the activation of Operation Sea Lion, his plan for the invasion of Britain. Before it could be launched, however, it was essential for the Luftwaffe to establish air supremacy over the English Channel and in the skies above southern England. This meant destroying RAF Fighter Command in the air and on the ground. Hitler's orders to Reichsmarschall Hermann Goering, commander-in-chief of the Luftwaffe, were unequivocal. The RAF, the Führer decreed, must be 'beaten down to such an extent that it can no longer muster any power of attack worth mentioning against the German crossing'. The ebullient Goering was bullishly confident that what Hitler had ordained could be achieved. He predicted that RAF Fighter Command would be smashed in four days.

The RAF, the Führer decreed, must be 'beaten down to such an extent that it can no longer muster any power of attack worth mentioning against the German crossing'.

Certainly, Goering had numbers on his side. The Luftwaffe had 900 fighters and 1,300 bombers ready for action at airfields in newly occupied France, the Low Countries and as far away as Norway. Air Chief Marshal Sir Hugh Dowding, Fighter Command's commander-in-chief, could put only 650 planes into the air. In some ways, however, the Luftwaffe's superiority was less marked than the RAF's numerical inferiority might imply. Though the Messerschmitt Bf 109, its main fighter plane, was as good as the Spitfires and better than the Hurricanes with which Fighter Command was equipped, its limited endurance meant it could spend only minutes in British air space before having to head home to refuel.

Above all, Fighter Command had radar to give it early warning of German attacks. There were 21 radar stations in all, stretched out in a vast arc along the coast. They were supported by 30,000 volunteer members of the Observer Corps, who manned 1,000 observation posts inland. Their plots were fed through to Fighter Command headquarters at Stanmore, Middlesex, to the four Group headquarters around the country and to any sectors under specific threat of attack. The Sector Controllers ordered the fighters up into the air and then used radio to help guide them to their targets.

THE BATTLE BEGINS

Hitler and Goering seemed in no hurry to launch their aerial attack. Though sporadic air combat began over the English Channel in July, it was not until 2 August that the long-awaited order went out 'to overpower the English air force in the shortest possible time'. The Luftwaffe prepared to take to the skies.

Goering's strategy was simple. It was to lure the RAF into combat by attacking targets Fighter Command would be

A veteran of the Battle of Britain, the Spitfire was among the aircraft that helped defeat the might of the German Luftwaffe.

forced to defend. Over the next weeks, the Luftwaffe's onslaught intensified. Starting on 13 August, its aircrews flew over 1,000 missions daily. Fighter Command shuddered under the successive blows, but it did not break. Instead, the Luftwaffe's bombers started to suffer mounting losses.

CHANGING TACTICS

Goering's immediate reaction was to change his tactics. Instead of allowing his Messerschmitts to roam over the aerial battlefield, he ordered them to stay close to the vulnerable bombers and protect them at all costs. He also decided to concentrate on knocking out Fighter Command's ground bases. This started to pay dividends. RAF losses mounted. Not only were its fighters being shot down, it was also losing pilots at an unsustainable rate. Then the Luftwaffe changed tactics again.

Hitler had given orders that London was not to be bombed, but on 24 August, a stray Luftwaffe bomber accidentally unloaded its bombs over the capital. The next night, RAF Bomber Command attacked Berlin. Goering had assured the Berliners that their city would never be bombed. In reprisal, Hitler ordered the Luftwaffe to switch targets. On the afternoon of 7 September, its bombers streamed towards London. The RAF's airfields had won the respite they needed.

THE TIDE TURNS

On 15 September, commemorated now as Battle of Britain Day, the Luftwaffe launched what it intended to be a knockout blow. More than 1,000 bombers, escorted by 700 fighters, set out to attack the capital. It ended in disaster even if RAF claims to have shot down 185 enemy aircraft were exaggerated. Fighter Command lost only 26 fighters and 13 pilots. Five days later, Hitler postponed Operation Sea Lion indefinitely. The tide had turned decisively in the RAF's favour. Over the next ten days – the last major daylight attack took place on 30 September – Fighter Command shot down more than double the number of aircraft it lost. Though it had come perilously close to losing the battle, it had clung on long enough to ensure victory.

The map shows the positioning of the British and German deployments during the Battle of Britain.

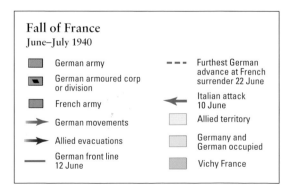

Fall of France
June–July 1940

▬ German army	▬ ▬ ▬ Furthest German advance at French surrender 22 June
◤ German armoured corp or division	
▬ French army	◀ Italian attack 10 June
→ German movements	▢ Allied territory
➤ Allied evacuations	▢ Germany and German occupied
▬ German front line 12 June	▢ Vichy France

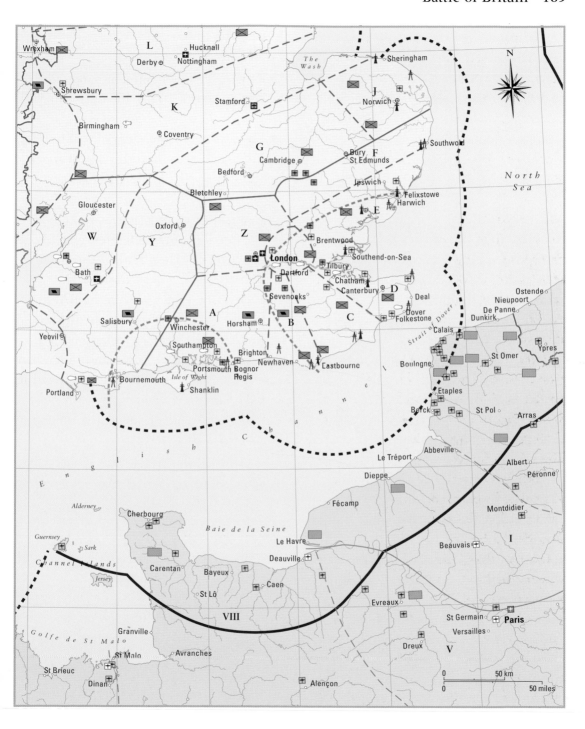

Battle of the Atlantic

STARTING ALMOST IMMEDIATELY AFTER THE OUTBREAK OF HOSTILITIES IN 1939, THE PROLONGED STRUGGLE FOR MASTERY OF THE ATLANTIC SHIPPING LANES WAS ONE OF THE MOST CRUCIAL BATTLES OF THE ENTIRE SECOND WORLD WAR.

Cutting Britain's vital supply lines across the Atlantic had been a German naval priority in the First World War. Yet, when hostilities broke out in 1939, Grand Admiral Karl Doenitz, the chief of the Kriegsmarine's U-boat arm, had only 57 submarines available and, of these, only eight were capable of cruising the Atlantic and making it back to home ports. Donitz told Hitler that he would need 300 ocean-going U-boats in order to mount a full-scale Atlantic campaign.

Despite this, the German submariners started their war with a bang. Only a few hours after hostilities commenced, U-30 sank the passenger liner *Athenia* en route to Montreal; 93 passengers and 19 members of the crew lost their lives. A fortnight later, U-29 sunk the aircraft carrier HMS *Courageous*. Then, on 13 October, U-47 managed to penetrate Scapa Flow, the Royal Navy's main anchorage, and sink the battleship HMS *Royal Oak*. Gunther Prien, the U-boat's commander,

and his crew received a hero's reception on their return to Kiel.

Over the coming months – even with the reintroduction of the convoy system – British merchant-shipping losses mounted steadily. By August 1940, 2.3 million tonnes (2.5 million tons) had been sunk. After the fall of France, Donitz had been able to shift many of his U-boats to ports on the Bay of Biscay, so enabling them to intensify their attacks.

In April 1941 alone, the U-boats sank some 635,029 tonnes (700,000 tons) of merchant shipping; by June, in what the U-boat commanders christened 'the happy time' – over five million tons had been lost. British shipyards were able to replace only 725,748 tonnes (800,000 tons) of the tonnage the U-boats had sunk.

THE 'WOLF PACKS' IN ACTION

The root of the problem was a shortage of escort vessels. Even though the United States supplied Britain with 50 antiquated destroyers, these did not fill the gap. Nor did existing aircraft have the range to provide air cover in the middle of the North Atlantic, where most of the sinkings took place.

Doenitz, too, had developed new tactics. Rather than deploying his growing U-boat strength singly, he devised the notion of 'wolf packs'. When a single U-boat sighted a convoy, instead of attacking it on its own as conventional practice dictated, it now shadowed it while radioing its position and course to other submarines in the area. Only when the 'wolf pack' had gathered did the U-boats strike – usually on the surface under cover of night.

When the United States entered the war in December 1941, the U-boats immediately took the conflict to the US Eastern Seaboard. The US Navy was unprepared for this and the resulting toll in shipping was substantial. Between January and April 1942, 80 ships were sunk; in April and May, the number of sinkings was triple what they had been at the start of the year. US countermeasures started to rectify the situation – most notably, the introduction of escort carriers to provide convoys with air protection. The balance began to shift in favour of the Allies as U-boat sinkings started to mount and the measures took effect.

An Enigma Machine. Cryptologists at Bletchley Park cracked the Enigma code, which was an important factor in determining the outcome of the Battle of the Atlantic.

CRISIS POINT

Doenitz was not beaten. In January 1943, the number of U-boats in daily operation averaged 116; by March, the number of ships sunk had risen to 1942 levels. It was little wonder that Churchill and Roosevelt, when meeting that January, made defeating the U-boat menace a top priority.

In May, the tide finally began to turn. Though convoy ONS2–42 was forced to battle no fewer than 51 U-boats between 28 April and 6 May, it managed to sink five of Doenitz's submarines for the loss of 13 of its 42 merchantmen. Three U-boats were sunk by the convoy's escorts and the remaining two by long-range flying boats. Together with Liberator bombers, these were a new weapon in the Allied armoury.

That same month, RAF Coastal Command mounted a combined air–sea offensive against the U-boats; in June the US Navy joined in, despatching hunter-killer groups of escort carriers and destroyers to attack the submarines. That was not all. Bletchley Park cryptologists had cracked the Kriegsmarine's version of the Enigma code and the introduction of airborne radar meant that the U-boats could be detected at night while travelling on the surface. In one month alone, 38 U-boats were sunk in the Bay of Biscay; 43 more were lost on patrol in Allied-dominated waters. As German losses became unsustainable, Doenitz ordered his submarines to withdraw from the North Atlantic. Though the U-boats kept fighting until the last hours of the war, the battle of the Atlantic ended with their total defeat.

The map shows the territories involved in the Battle of the Atlantic, as well as the extent of air cover and major convoy routes.

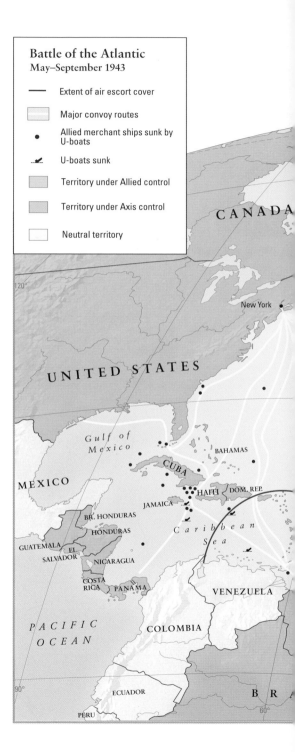

Battle of the Atlantic
May–September 1943

— Extent of air escort cover

Major convoy routes

• Allied merchant ships sunk by U-boats

U-boats sunk

Territory under Allied control

Territory under Axis control

Neutral territory

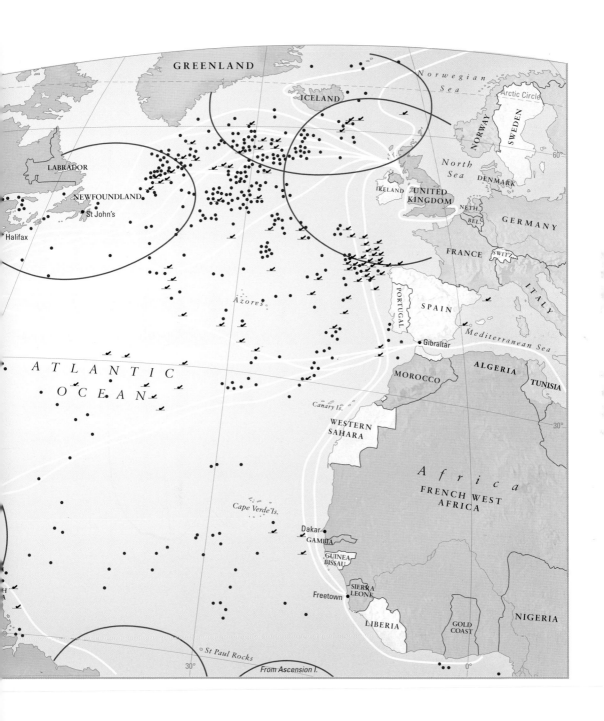

GREENLAND

Norwegian Sea

ICELAND

Arctic Circle

NORWAY

SWEDEN

LABRADOR

60°

NEWFOUNDLAND

St John's

North Sea

IRELAND

UNITED KINGDOM

DENMARK

NETH.

BEL.

GERMANY

Halifax

FRANCE

SWITZ.

ITALY

Azores

PORTUGAL

SPAIN

Mediterranean Sea

Gibraltar

A T L A N T I C

O C E A N

ALGERIA

TUNISIA

MOROCCO

Canary Is.

WESTERN SAHARA

30°

A f r i c a

FRENCH WEST AFRICA

Cape Verde Is.

Dakar

GAMBIA

GUINEA BISSAU

SIERRA LEONE

Freetown

NIGERIA

LIBERIA

GOLD COAST

St Paul Rocks

30°

0°

From Ascension I.

Pearl Harbor

WHEN JAPANESE AIRCRAFT STRUCK AT PEARL HARBOR, IT WAS HISTORY'S GREATEST-EVER SURPRISE ATTACK. THOUGH MOST OF THE US PACIFIC FLEET WAS PUT OUT OF ACTION, ITS AIRCRAFT CARRIERS, WHICH WERE AT SEA AT THE TIME, ESCAPED.

Pearl Harbor had been a hub of US naval power in the Pacific ever since King Kalakua, the ruler of the Hawaiian Islands, had given the United States the right to develop a coaling station there in 1887. In 1941, it had been designated the US Pacific Fleet's new home base. As such, it was a logical place for the Japanese to attack. Their aim, though ambitious, was simple. It was to eliminate US naval power in the Pacific by launching a devastating knockout surprise blow while the United States was still unready for war.

YAMAMOTO PREPARES

Relations between the two powers had been deteriorating for months as the United States embargoed supplying Japan with vital strategic war materials. Prohibiting the selling of oil and aviation fuel to the Japanese was the final straw. Though personally opposed to the prospect of waging war against the United States, Admiral Isoruko Yamamoto, commander of Japan's Combined Fleet, had already started formulating a scheme for the Pearl Harbor attack. Lieutenant-Commander Minoru Genda, Japan's leading aerial tactician, was put in charge of detailed operational planning; Lieutenant-Commander Mitsuo Fuchida, the Japanese Navy's top air ace, was chosen to lead the actual assault.

The first difficulty was Pearl Harbor's relative shallowness. With an average depth of only 13.7 metres (45 feet), it was considered safe from torpedo-bomber attack, since the Japanese torpedoes required more than 23 metres (75 feet) of depth to run effectively. The Japanese got over the problem by devising a shallow-running torpedo that would more or less skim the surface of the water after being released from a low-flying aeroplane. Months of rigorous training with this new innovation followed until Fuchida's pilots were ready to go. It looked as if war was fast becoming inevitable.

'CLIMB MOUNT NIITAKA'

In late autumn 1941, the Pearl Harbor task force secretly assembled in Tankan Bay in northern Japan. It consisted of 32 vessels: the aircraft carriers *Akagi*, *Hiryu*, *Soryu*, *Kaga*, *Zuikaku* and *Shokaku*, plus supporting battleships, heavy cruisers, destroyers and a flotilla of screening submarines. Vice-Admiral Chuichi Nagumo was in command. On 26 November, his fleet weighed anchor and sailed, taking the northern route towards Hawaii. Even though the weather and seas were rough, the Japanese believed that the winter storms would mask their approach and lessen the chances of a premature enemy encounter.

For the same reason, the task force observed strict radio silence. On 2 December, however, Nagumo received a coded message from Tokyo. It read simply 'Climb Mount Niitaka'. It was the signal for the attack to go ahead.

'TORA, TORA, TORA!'

By 6 December, the Japanese were 370 km (230 miles) to the north of Oahu, well within striking distance of Pearl Harbor. At 6 am precisely the following morning, the carriers turned into the wind and launched the first wave of attacking aeroplanes. It was led by Fuchida himself. The second wave followed an hour later, by which time Fuchida was well on the way to his target.

That Sunday morning, the US forces at Pearl Harbor were totally unprepared for war. The fleet lay peacefully at anchor in the harbour, while, rather than being dispersed, the base's protecting fighters sat parked neatly wing to wing on the nearby airfields. Though a newly installed radar station had detected Fuchida's approach, his aeroplanes were mistaken for a flight of US B-17 bombers expected from California that morning. Pearl Harbor lay completely open to attack.

Fuchida struck at 7.55 am. Within 15 minutes, his torpedo-bombers had managed to sink five US battleships and badly damage three more, while swarms of fighters and dive bombers struck the airfields at Kaneohe, Hickam, Ewa, Bellows and Wheeler, catching the Americans on the ground. The second wave, which arrived at around 8.50 am, continued the attack, still virtually unopposed. At 9.45 am, the Japanese brought their assault to an end. In all, they lost only 29 aircraft out of the 360 that had been launched from Nagumo's carriers. He decided that he had done enough. He cancelled the planned third strike, which would have inflicted even more damage on the Americans, and instructed the task force to make for home.

Despite appearances, the Japanese had not achieved complete success. The Pacific Fleet's three aircraft carriers, which initially had been the Japanese priority target, were at sea when the torpedo bombers struck and so escaped unscathed. Had Nagumo launched a third strike, as Fuchida and Genda both advocated, they, too, might have been located and sunk. By failing to attack and destroy Pearl Harbor's vast oil storage bunkers, the Japanese also missed the opportunity to put the Pacific Fleet out of action for months. They were to pay dearly for both oversights.

Japanese aircraft attacking Pearl Harbor in December 1941. It was history's greatest-ever surprise attack.

Japanese Attack on Pearl Harbor
7 December 1941

1 Fifteen Kate high-level bombers from the *Akagi*, the first of 49 bombers to attack the four ships successively

2 Kate torpedo bombers from the *Soryu*

3 Kate torpedo bombers from the *Hiryu*

4 Lead Kate torpedo bombers from the *Akagi* and *Kaga*

5 Follow-up Kate torpedo bombers from the *Soryu* and *Hiryu*

1. Tender *Whitney* and destroyers *Tucker, Conyngham, Reid, Case* and *Selfridge*
2. Destroyer *Blue*
3. Light cruiser *Phoenix*
4. Destroyers *Aylwin, Farragut, Dale* and *Monaghan*
5. Destroyers *Patterson, Ralph, Talbot* and *Henley*
6. Tender *Dobbin* and destroyers *Worden, Hull, Dewey, Phelps* and *MacDonough*
7. Hospital Ship *Solace*
8. Destroyer *Allen*
9. Destroyer *Chew*
10. Destroyer minesweepers *Gamble* and *Montgomery* and light minelayer *Ramsay*
11. Destroyer minesweepers *Trever, Breese, Zane, Perry* and *Wasmuth*
12. Repair vessel *Medusa*
13. Seaplane tender *Curtiss*
14. Light cruiser *Detroit*
15. Light cruiser *Raleigh*
16. Target battleship *Utah*
17. Seaplane tender *Tangier*
18. Battleship *Nevada*
19. Battleship *Arizona*
20. Repair vessel *Vestal*
21. Battleship *Tennessee*
22. Battleship *West Virginia*
23. Battleship *Maryland*
24. Battleship *Oklahoma*
25. Oiler *Neosho*
26. Battleship *California*
27. Seaplane tender *Avocet*
28. Destroyer *Shaw*
29. Destroyer *Downes*
30. Destroyer *Cassin*
31. Battleship *Pennsylvania*
32. Submarine *Cachalot*
33. Minelayer *Oglala*
34. Light cruiser *Helena*
35. Auxiliary vessel *Argonne*
36. Gunboat *Sacramento*
37. Destroyer *Jarvis*
38. Destroyer *Mugford*
39. Seaplane tender *Swan*
40. Repair vessel *Rigel*
41. Oiler *Ramapo*
42. Heavy cruiser *New Orleans*
43. Destroyer *Cummings* and light minelayers *Preble* and *Tracy*
44. Heavy cruiser *San Francisco*
45. Destroyer minesweeper *Grebe*, destroyer *Schley* and light minelayers *Pruitt* and *Sicard*
46. Light cruiser *Honolulu*
47. Light cruiser *St. Louis*
48. Destroyer *Bagley*
49. Submarines *Narwhal, Dolphin* and *Tautog* and tenders *Thornton* and *Hulbert*
50. Submarine tender *Pelias*
51. Auxiliary vessel *Sumner*
52. Auxiliary vessel *Castor*

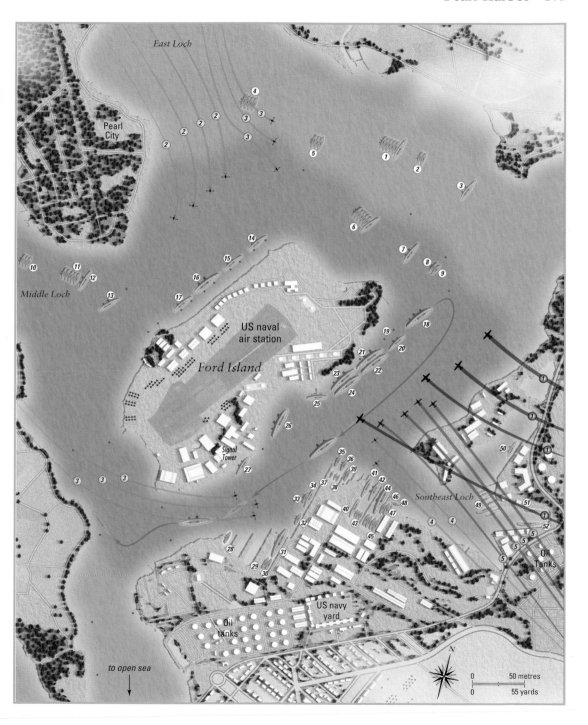

Midway

IN WHAT WAS ONE OF THE MOST DECISIVE NAVAL BATTLES OF ALL TIME, TWO US NAVY TASK FORCES, THOUGH OUTGUNNED AND UNDER STRENGTH, TURNED THE TABLES ON THE JAPANESE TO END THEIR NAVAL DOMINANCE OF THE PACIFIC.

Fresh from their triumph at Pearl Harbor, Japan's crack fleet of aircraft carriers rampaged through the Pacific until their progress was checked in the Coral Sea. In the first carrier battle of the Pacific war, they lost more aeroplanes than the Americans, but the latter lost more ships than the Japanese. The carrier *Lexington* was sunk and *Yorktown* was heavily damaged.

Logic dictated that the Japanese carriers should return to their home ports to refit. That may well have been Yamamoto's intention, but then, even before the Coral Sea action, an unexpected event changed his mind. On 18 April 1942, Lieutenant-Colonel James Doolittle led 16 US Army B-25B Mitchell bombers in an air raid on Tokyo.

Though the damage the bombers inflicted was minimal, the psychological shock was immense. The mortified Yamamoto began planning another assault. This time, the target was Midway, a strategically important island in the mid-Pacific.

A REVENGE ASSAULT

Yamamoto's plan was a complex one. One battle group would mount a diversionary raid on the Aleutian Islands. The Midway Occupation Force would sail from the Marianas to Midway, where it would rendezvous with the main battle fleet under Yamamoto himself. Vice-Admiral Chuichi Nagumo's First Carrier Striking Force would sail for Midway, ahead of Yamamoto, to provide air support. Finally, a submarine screen would deploy between Midway and Pearl Harbor to intercept any US naval force putting to sea.

> *Though the damage the bombers inflicted was minimal, the psychological shock was immense. The mortified Yamamoto began planning another assault.*

Because the Japanese were so widely dispersed, only the carriers and the main battle fleet could support each other. It also meant that Yamamoto was forced to transmit his orders by radio. He was unaware of the fact that American cryptologists had cracked the Japanese

naval code and so were able to identify Midway as the target. Admiral Chester Nimitz, the commander of the US Pacific

The map shows the movements made by the United States and by the Japanese during the Battle of Midway.

Battle of Midway
4–5 June 1942

➤ US fleet movements   ▪▪➤ Japanese air strikes

▪▪➤ US air strikes   ✳ Ship damaged

➤ Japanese fleet movements   ✸ Ship sunk

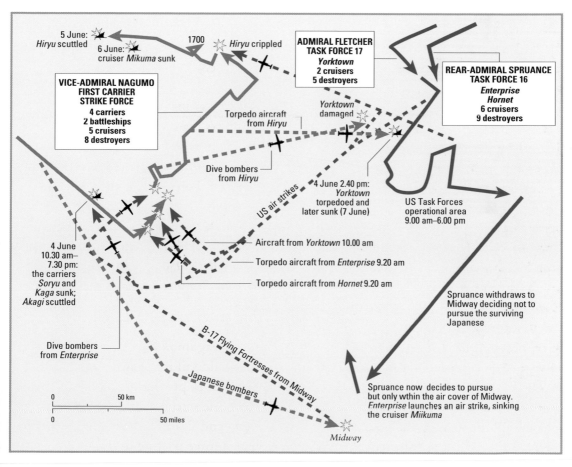

5 June: *Hiryu* scuttled
6 June: cruiser *Mikuma* sunk
1700   *Hiryu* crippled

ADMIRAL FLETCHER TASK FORCE 17
Yorktown
2 cruisers
5 destroyers

REAR-ADMIRAL SPRUANCE TASK FORCE 16
Enterprise
Hornet
6 cruisers
9 destroyers

VICE-ADMIRAL NAGUMO FIRST CARRIER STRIKE FORCE
4 carriers
2 battleships
5 cruisers
8 destroyers

Torpedo aircraft from *Hiryu*

Yorktown damaged

Dive bombers from *Hiryu*

US air strikes

4 June 2.40 pm: *Yorktown* torpedoed and later sunk (7 June)

US Task Forces operational area 9.00 am–6.00 pm

4 June 10.30 am–7.30 pm: the carriers *Soryu* and *Kaga* sunk; *Akagi* scuttled

Aircraft from *Yorktown* 10.00 am

Torpedo aircraft from *Enterprise* 9.20 am

Torpedo aircraft from *Hornet* 9.20 am

Spruance withdraws to Midway deciding not to pursue the surviving Japanese

Dive bombers from *Enterprise*

B-17 Flying Fortresses from Midway

Japanese bombers

0   50 km
0   50 miles

Spruance now decides to pursue but only wthin the air cover of Midway. *Enterprise* launches an air strike, sinking the cruiser *Miikuma*

Midway

Fleet, made his dispositions accordingly. His ships – divided into two task forces commanded by Rear-Admiral Raymond Spruance and Rear-Admiral Frank Fletcher – sailed from Pearl Harbor before the Japanese submarine screen could take up station. Their orders were to take up position north-east of Midway and ambush the Japanese carriers when they arrived.

NAGUMO STRIKES

Nagumo launched his first strike at Midway at 4.30 am on 4 June 1942. He believed that one attack would be enough to knock out the island's defences, but he was soon disillusioned. As his aeroplanes powered towards their target, US fighters scrambled to intercept them, while land-based bombers counter-attacked his fleet.

Though the latter were driven off without inflicting any damage, the air commander signalled that a second land strike would be needed. Nagumo ordered his remaining planes to be rearmed with incendiary and fragmentation bombs.

THE US COUNTER-STRIKE

Nagumo was still unaware that the US carriers were approaching, though his scouting aeroplanes had reported sighting some American ships 322 km (200 miles) or so away. It was not until 8.20 am that he received accurate intelligence. The terse message read 'Enemy force is accompanied by what appears to be a carrier'. It was Fletcher's task force closing for action.

Nagumo hesitated. The second wave's rearming for land attack was almost complete. Now it would have to be rearmed again. Also, his fighters were running low on fuel, and he had to recover his first wave. The result was confusion. As Nagumo altered course eastwards to meet the new threat, the flight decks of his carriers were crowded with aeroplanes, some rearming, some refuelling and others waiting for the chance to launch.

At 9.30 am, the first wave of American torpedo bombers located Nagumo's carriers. A second one followed ten minutes later. Both were intercepted by Nagumo's fighter umbrella and almost all of them were shot down without scoring a single hit. Then, just as the last of them were falling from the skies, the American dive bombers arrived on the scene. At 10.22 am they attacked the *Kagu* and then *Soryu* and *Akagi*. Within minutes, all three carriers had been put out of action. They eventually sank.

Only the *Hiryu* was left to continue the battle. Believing that he was fighting only one US carrier, Nagumo ordered its

The map shows the movements of Japanese and US naval fleets and aircraft during the Battle of Midway.

aircraft to attack *Yorktown*. They damaged the carrier so badly that Fletcher had to abandon her. She was later sunk by a Japanese submarine. *Hiryu*, however, was not to escape. Late in the afternoon, she was attacked by US dive bombers and set on fire. She was scuttled the following day.

The defeat was as total as it was devastating. In one day, the Japanese had lost their entire fleet carrier force and, with it, their naval command of the Pacific. The strategic balance shifted inexorably towards the United States.

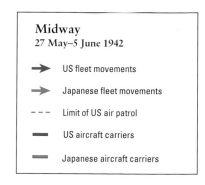

Midway
27 May–5 June 1942

→ US fleet movements

→ Japanese fleet movements

--- Limit of US air patrol

▬ US aircraft carriers

▬ Japanese aircraft carriers

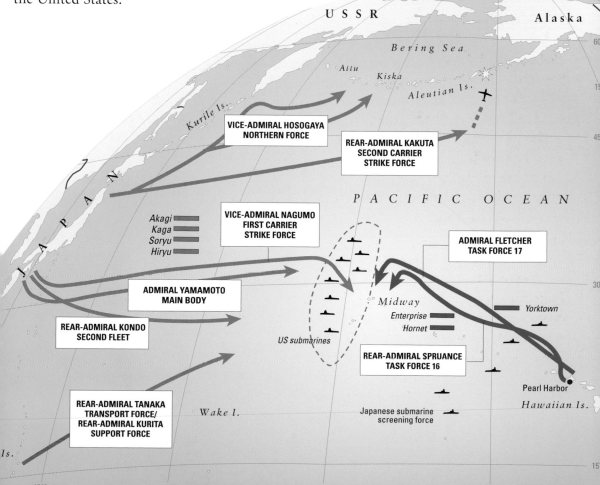

El Alamein

Montgomery's decisive victory over **R**ommel in **N**orth **A**frica in **O**ctober 1942 finally turned the desert war firmly in **B**ritain's favour. **T**he vaunted **A**frika **K**orps was forced out of **E**gypt and into headlong retreat.

It was Britain's darkest hour in the protracted North African campaign its 8th Army had been waging ever since the Italians entered the war in 1940. Between January and July 1942, the British were driven back relentlessly into Egypt by General Erwin Rommel's combined German and Italian forces. Eventually, the 8th Army took up position at El Alamein. If Rommel broke through again, there would be nothing to stop him reaching Cairo and the Suez Canal. It was a stark choice between finally stopping the 'Desert Fox' in his tracks and ignominious defeat.

What the British were unaware of at the time was that the seemingly unstoppable Rommel had outrun his supplies. Indeed, Field Marshal Albert Kesselring, the overall German commander in the Mediterranean, had ordered him to halt the Axis advance, only to be ignored. Rommel, who had now been promoted to field marshal, went over his head and appealed directly to Hitler. The Führer allowed him to continue to thrust forwards.

> *If Rommel broke through, there was nothing to stop him reaching Cairo and the Suez Canal. It was a stark choice between stopping the 'Desert Fox' and defeat...*

CHANGING COMMANDERS

General Sir Claude Auchinleck, British commander-in-chief in the Middle East, resolved to make a stand at Alam el Halfa, to the south of El Alamein. When Rommel attacked there, he lacked the strength to break through and was checked, if not actually repulsed. It was not enough to save Auchinleck and General Neil Ritchie, the 8th Army's field commander, from the consequences of defeat. Churchill, who had flown to Cairo himself to assess the situation, sacked them both. General Sir Harold Alexander took over from Auchinleck; Ritchie's successor was General Sir Bernard Montgomery.

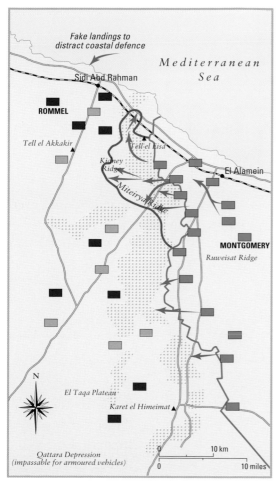

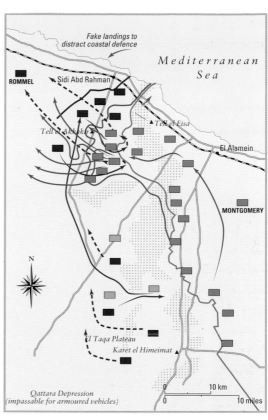

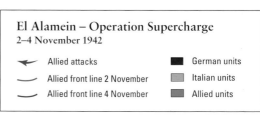

El Alamein – Operation Supercharge
2–4 November 1942

← Allied attacks	■ German units
⌒ Allied front line 2 November	■ Italian units
⌒ Allied front line 4 November	■ Allied units

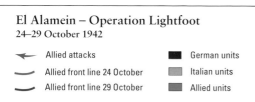

El Alamein – Operation Lightfoot
24–29 October 1942

← Allied attacks	■ German units
⌒ Allied front line 24 October	■ Italian units
⌒ Allied front line 29 October	■ Allied units

The maps show the positioning of the German, Italian and Allied units and the Allied attacks at El Alamein in 1942.

Montgomery was actually Churchill's second choice – his first, General William 'Strafer' Gott, had been shot down and killed on his way to take over the command. Nor had he any previous experience of desert warfare. Nevertheless, he was supremely confident that he would succeed. He told his troops that there would be 'no more belly-aching and no more retreats'. Having skilfully repelled a second Axis attack at Alam el Halfa at the end of August, Monty began to build up the material supremacy he needed for his own offensive to begin.

'HIT THE ENEMY FOR SIX!'

Despite pressure from Churchill to bring the date of the attack forwards, Montgomery stubbornly refused to move until he was absolutely ready. By October, he had 150,000 men ready for action plus 1,114 tanks. Rommel could muster 110,000 men, but only 600 tanks fit to take the field.

The attack began late in the evening of 23 October, when Montgomery's artillery opened fire along a 10 km (6 mile) front stretching from the Mediterranean coast inland. The plan was for 13th Corps to make a diversionary attack in the south to pin down the armour of the 21st Panzer and Italian Ariete divisions. Shortly afterwards, 30th Corps's infantry would advance in the north, clearing two narrow corridors through the formidable minefields in front of the Axis positions. The armoured divisions of 10th Corps would drive through the gaps the infantry had opened up for them.

Rommel won the nickname 'Desert Fox' through his exploits in North Africa. The most charismatic of Hitler's generals, he was admired by many of his enemies, including Montgomery and Patton.

Progress was slow. Rather than achieving a quick breakthrough, the 8th Army faced a slogging match. Montgomery's aim was now to lure the best Axis units to a part of the battlefield where they could be worn down by constant pressure from his superior forces. He called the process 'crumbling'.

Though Rommel, who had been absent on sick leave in Germany when the battle started, put up a spirited resistance when he returned to take up command, this was exactly what happened. After suspending activity in the south, Montgomery threw all his weight into the coastal area. Allied air superiority, shortages of fuel, lack of replacement parts and machinery as well as dwindling supplies of ammunition all compounded Rommel's problems.

CRUSHING THE AFRIKA KORPS

The decisive breakthrough finally came on 2 November, when the 2nd New Zealand Division and the 1st Armoured Division attacked in the north at Kidney Ridge. They broke through the Axis defences, forcing Rommel to commit his last reserves. In the ensuing tank battle, the Axis forces lost more than 100 tanks; Rommel was left with only 35 tanks capable of further action.

Realizing that the battle was lost, Rommel asked Hitler's permission to withdraw. The Führer ordered him to stand his ground and fight to the last man. With a 19-km (12-mile) gap opening in his line, Rommel ignored Hitler's orders. The Afrika Korps abandoned its Italian allies and began to retreat west.

It was the turning point of the long drawn-out desert campaign. Montgomery's crushing victory not only saved Egypt and the Suez Canal, it was the first major defeat the Wehrmacht had suffered outside Russia since the start of the war. The Desert Fox had been defeated. Later on, Rommel would become embroiled in a plot to overthrow Hitler and was given a choice – court marshal and disgrace or suicide. He chose suicide in exchange for the lives of his wife and son.

FACT FILE
El Alamein

Date: October–November 1942

Location: El Alamein, Egypt

Context: The Second World War (1939–1945)

States Involved: UK; Germany, Italy

Commanders and Leaders: Harold Alexander, Bernard Montgomery (UK); Erwin Rommel, Georg Stumme, Ettore Bastico (Germany/Italy)

Outcome: Decisive Allied victory

Aftermath: Finally turned the desert war firmly in Britain's favour; the Afrika Korps was forced out of Egypt

Stalingrad

WHEN FIELD MARSHAL FRIEDRICH VON PAULUS AND THE REMAINS OF THE CRACK GERMAN SIXTH ARMY SURRENDERED TO THE RUSSIANS AFTER A PROTRACTED SIEGE, IT WAS THE TURNING POINT OF THE WAR ON THE EASTERN FRONT.

Despite the horrendous losses his armies had suffered on the Eastern Front in winter 1941, Hitler was determined to return to the offensive the next summer. This time, instead of striking towards Moscow again, he attacked in the south with the aims of seizing the Caucasian oilfields and capturing the strategically important city of Stalingrad on the river Volga. His generals cautioned that his forces were not strong enough to take both objectives. He overruled them. Capturing the oil fields was vital. If he did not gain control of them, he would have to consider ending the war. As for Stalingrad, it was not only an important transportation hub and industrial centre. Because it was named after the Soviet dictator Joseph Stalin, its fall would deal a crippling blow to Russian morale.

Many believed that Paulus should try to break out of the encirclement. Hitler thought differently. He refused point-blank to countenance a retreat.

THE DRIVE TO THE VOLGA

The offensive started in June 1942. At first, everything went as Hitler had predicted. Sevastopol in the Crimea was captured, then Rostov fell. It was then that the over-confident Führer made the first of a series of blunders that would bring about catastrophic defeat.

Angered by what he considered to be inadequate progress, Hitler divided Army Group South into two separate groups – Army Group A and Army Group B. Army Group A was tasked with capturing the oilfields. Army Group B was ordered to take Stalingrad and protect Army Group A's flank. The problem was that the Führer constantly changed his mind about which attack was to have priority. Thus, the 4th Panzer Army found itself being switched from one front to the other and then back again. To compound the error, Hitler ordered the 11th Army, his only substantial reserve, north to reinforce the Leningrad front.

THE GERMAN ASSAULT

In spite of all these problems, the 6th Army reached the river Volga north of the city on 23 August. It was not until 13 September, however, that General Friedrich von Paulus, commander of the 6th Army, was ready to start pushing into the heart of Stalingrad itself. He was supported by the 4th Panzer Army, which attacked the southern suburbs.

The attacks were fiercely opposed. Marshal Vasily Chuikov, commander of the 62nd Army, organized a stubborn street-by-street resistance. Slowly, continuous German pressure forced the Russians back. By 12 October, Paulus had reached the centre of the city – or what remained of it. He then attacked the northern factory district. It took him until 18 November to reach the Volga there.

Paulus had won control of 90 per cent of the city, but at a massive cost. In order to reinforce the 6th Army, a fateful decision was taken to substitute Romanian troops to defend its ever-extending flanks. The Russian high command judged that the time had come to launch a full-scale counter-attack.

THE RUSSIAN OFFENSIVE

On 19 and 20 November, the Russians launched massive attacks to the north and south of Stalingrad. Three armies powered their way across the river Don. Breaking through the luckless Romanians, they raced to link up and encircle the 6th Army. The besiegers had become the besieged.

Many believed that Paulus should try to break out of the encirclement. Hitler thought differently. He refused point-blank to countenance a retreat. Instead, he ordered Paulus to hold his ground and await relief. In the meantime, Goering assured the Führer that the Luftwaffe would be able to supply Paulus by air.

The ebullient but incompetent Reichsmarschal was incorrect. The Luftwaffe was not up to the task. Theoretically, the maximum tonnage it could deliver to Paulus was just over 117 tons per day as opposed to the 800 tons required. As the Russian grip tightened remorselessly, the Germans began to starve. Lacking winter clothing, many German soldiers froze to death. Meanwhile, Hitler ordered Field Marshal Erich von Manstein to break the siege. Manstein got to within 48 km (30 miles) of the city, but on 19 December he was forced into retreat.

On 8 January 1943, the Russians began an all-out assault. Hitler ordered Paulus to fight to the last man. On 30 January – five days after the last airfield in the German-held 'hedgehog' had been overrun – he made him a field marshal, reasoning that, as no German officer of that rank had ever surrendered, Paulus would kill himself rather than capitulate.

The Führer was mistaken. The next day, following its commander's capture, the bulk of what was left of the 6th Army laid down its arms and surrendered. The last German resistance ceased on 2 February. The long months of bitter fighting were finally at their disastrous end.

FACT FILE

Stalingrad

Date: 23 August 1942–2 February 1943

Location: Stalingrad, Soviet Union

Context: The Second World War (1939–1945)

States Involved: Soviet Union; Germany

Commanders and Leaders: Georgy Zhukov, Nicolay Voronov (Soviet Union); Erich von Manstein, Friedrich Paulus (Germany)

Outcome: Decisive Soviet victory

Aftermath: Turning point in the war. Germany secured no further strategic victories in the East.

The map shows the movements made by the Germans and by the Soviets during the Battle for Stalingrad.

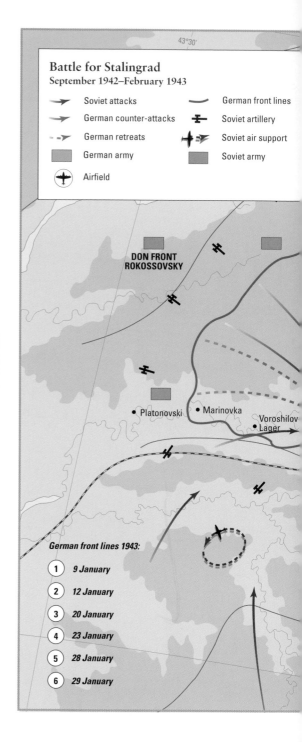

43°30'

Battle for Stalingrad
September 1942–February 1943

→ Soviet attacks
→ German counter-attacks
⇢ German retreats
▭ German army
✈ Airfield

⌒ German front lines
⊣⊢ Soviet artillery
⊣✈ Soviet air support
▭ Soviet army

DON FRONT
ROKOSSOVSKY

• Platonovski   • Marinovka
                 • Voroshilov
                   Lager

German front lines 1943:

(1) 9 January

(2) 12 January

(3) 20 January

(4) 23 January

(5) 28 January

(6) 29 January

Don

Kotluban

Samofalovka

Erzovka

44°30'

49°

0   10 km

0   10 miles

N

1

Sovkhov Nol

Kuzmichi

Borodkin

3

Orlovka

Vinnovka

Rynok

Malaya Rossoshka

Novaya Nadezhda

Spartakovka

Baburkin

4

1

Gorodishche

Novo-alekseyevski

3

Gumrak

5

vka

Pitomnik

5

Stalingrad

Volga

Stavenki

PAULUS

6

Krasnaya Sloboda

Burkauski

2

Yelshanka

Kuperosnoye

Tsybenko

Yelkhi

Straya Otrada

STALINGRAD FRONT
YEREMENKO

Varvarovka

Kursk

STILL THE GREATEST TANK BATTLE EVER FOUGHT, KURSK WAS THE LAST MAJOR OFFENSIVE LAUNCHED BY HITLER'S WEHRMACHT ON THE EASTERN FRONT DURING THE SECOND WORLD WAR. IT ENDED IN TOTAL VICTORY FOR THE RUSSIANS.

After their crushing defeat at Stalingrad and the subsequent Russian advance westwards, Hitler and his generals began debating how best to go about regaining the strategic initiative on the Eastern Front. Some – Guderian and Manstein – argued that by adopting a strategy of dynamic mobile defence, the Wehrmacht could still inflict crippling losses on the Russians in a series of localized clashes. General Kurt Zeitzler, the German Army's chief of staff, called for the launch of another all-out summer offensive. He believed that by employing every available tank, the German panzer divisions could still annihilate the opposing Russian armour in one decisive battle.

The place Zeitzler proposed for the great confrontation was the Kursk salient, a huge bulge in the Eastern Front jutting into German-held territory almost halfway between Moscow and the Black Sea. His plan was to pinch out the salient by launching an armoured pincer movement against it, thrusting from north and south simultaneously. He christened it 'Operation Citadel'. Hitler endorsed the plan in early May 1943 and the offensive opened exactly two months later.

PREPARING FOR THE OFFENSIVE

The German high command prepared meticulously for the attack. The 9th Army, commanded by General Walther Model and consisting of four panzer and one infantry corps, would spearhead the northern thrust. General Hermann Hoth's 4th Panzer Army and Army Detachment Kempf formed the southern pincer. The Germans fielded 2,700 tanks and assault guns, 1,800 aircraft and 900,000 troops.

Though these figures were impressive, the Germans were still at a disadvantage. The new Panther and Tiger super-tanks, on which they were relying to break through the eight Russian defence lines in the salient and then crush the opposing armour, were untried in action. The anti-tank defences the Luftwaffe had detected were so formidable that one German general warned that a direct tank assault on them could turn out to be a ride to death. The Russians had numerical and material superiority with 3,600 tanks, 2,400 aircraft, 20,000 artillery pieces and a staggering 1,300,000 men.

Hitler was undeterred. He insisted that the attack go ahead. Had he known that Russian spies inside the Reich had succeeded in getting full details of Operation Citadel through to Moscow, he might have decided otherwise.

A FIGHT TO THE FINISH

The battle began on 4 July. In the north, the 9th Army soon ran into trouble. Despite Model's best efforts, it became bogged down in a war of attrition it could not hope to win. By 10 July, it had managed to advance only 10 km (6 miles) at the cost of 25,000 lives, 200 tanks destroyed and 200 aircraft shot down. Even though Army Group Centre committed all its available reserves in support, Model's men found it impossible to break through the Russian defences.

Things went better for Manstein in the south. He managed to drive a wedge 40 km (25 miles) into the salient. By 11 July, Hoth's 4th Panzer Army was in a position to secure a bridgehead over the river Psel, capture the town of Prokhorovka and push forwards to Oboyan and then on to Kursk itself.

The assault on Prokhorovka was led by SS General Paul Hauser and his 2nd SS Panzer Corps, which consisted of three crack Panzergrenadier divisions. Opposing him was the newly arrived 5th Guards Tank Army, commanded by Lieutenant-General Pavel Rotmistrov. The resulting battle ended in a draw with both sides suffering substantial tank losses.

Hitler intervened. Manstein argued to be allowed to continue the attack, but Hilter ordered the 2nd SS Panzer Corps to be dispersed, ready to deal with anticipated Russian counter-attacks elsewhere. Then, faced with dealing with the invasion of Sicily by the Western Allies, which began the same day that Hauser started his attack, he decided to call off the offensive completely. The Russians counter-attacked immediately. By 23 July, the Germans had been forced right back to their starting lines and by 5 August, the Russian forces had made substantial gains on either side of the salient. The retreat turned into rout as the Germans fell back further. Kharkov was captured by the Russians on 23 August; by 18 August the Orel salient had been eliminated. For the rest of the war, the Wehrmacht in the East was to lurch from defeat to defeat.

The map below shows the movements made by the Germans and by the Soviets during Kursk – Operation Citadel.

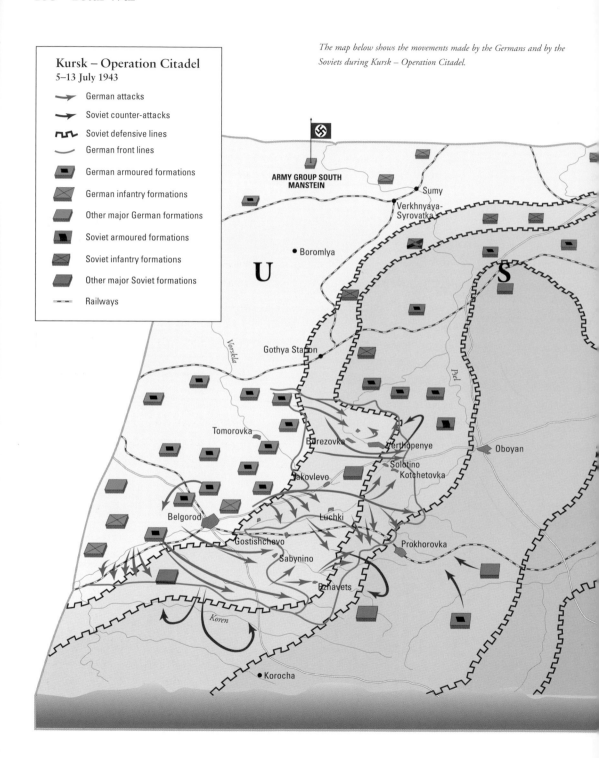

Kursk – Operation Citadel
5–13 July 1943

German attacks

Soviet counter-attacks

Soviet defensive lines

German front lines

German armoured formations

German infantry formations

Other major German formations

Soviet armoured formations

Soviet infantry formations

Other major Soviet formations

Railways

ARMY GROUP SOUTH
MANSTEIN

Sumy

Verkhnyaya-
Syrovatka

U

Boromlya

S

Vorskla

Gothya Station

Psel

Tomorovka

Berezovka

Verthopenye

Oboyan

Solotino
Kotchetovka

Yakovlevo

Belgorod

Luchki

Prokhorovka

Gostishchevo

Sabynino

Dzhavets

Koren

Korocha

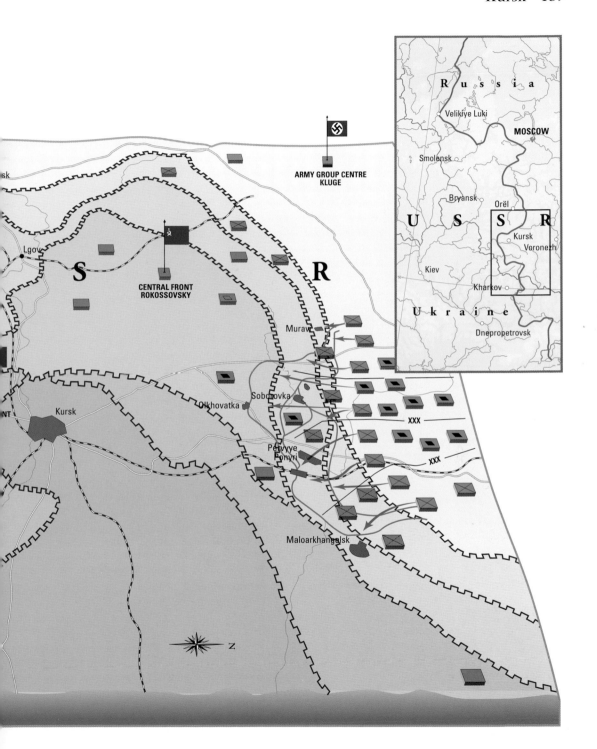

sk

Lgov

S

CENTRAL FRONT
ROKOSSOVSKY

ARMY GROUP CENTRE
KLUGE

R

Murav

Sobomovka

Olkhovatka

Kursk

Petvyye
Ponyri

NT

Maloarkhangelsk

XXX

XXX

Z

Russia

Velikiye Luki

MOSCOW

Smolensk

Bryansk

Orël

U   **S**   **S**   **R**

Kursk
Voronezh

Kiev

Kharkov

Ukraine

Dnepropetrovsk

D-Day

ALMOST AS SOON AS THE BRITISH WERE FORCED OFF THE EUROPEAN CONTINENT AT DUNKIRK IN 1940, THEY BEGAN PLANNING FOR AN EVENTUAL RETURN. IN JANUARY 1943, THE ALLIES COMMITTED THEMSELVES TO A MAJOR LANDING IN FRANCE.

The landing in France, which had been agreed to under pressure from the United States, now began to take shape. Planning for what was code named Operation Overlord swiftly moved forwards into top gear. The landings, when they occurred, would be the biggest amphibious operation ever launched. Eschewing the most direct invasion route across the Straits of Dover, the planners opted instead to land in Normandy. Although further from Germany than the Pas de Calais, its long sandy beaches were sheltered from the prevailing south-west winds by the Cotentin Peninsula. It also possessed two major ports – Cherbourg and Le Havre.

THE ALLIED PLAN

The plan was to land on five beaches on the Normandy coast, preceding these landings by dropping glider-borne troops to secure the flanks of the bridgehead. The US 1st Army, with General Omar Bradley in command, was to land on Utah and Omaha beaches. The British 2nd Army and the 3rd Canadian Division, both commanded by General Miles Dempsey, was to land on Juno, Sword and Gold beaches, further along the coast.

General Dwight D. Eisenhower was in overall command, with General Sir Bernard Montgomery in immediate charge of the troops on the ground. The total fighting strength was 45 divisions and a combined strength of nearly a million men. A further million staffed the vast logistical tail needed to support the combatants. The landing forces would be supported by massive naval and air formations, which, again, numbered another million men.

To face the invasion, Field Marshal Karl von Rundstedt, the German commander-in-chief in the West, had 10 panzer, 12 infantry and 31 coastal defence divisions. Though this looked impressive, only some of it – three panzer divisions, two infantry divisions, four coastal defence divisions and the garrison of Cherbourg – was defending the actual invasion area. The rest of Army Group B, commanded by Field Marshal Erwin Rommel, was defending the Pas de Calais at Hitler's insistence. The Führer had been fooled by a comprehensive Allied deception plan. He was sure that the real blow would fall there and any landing elsewhere would be a feint. He also took direct charge of the panzer reserves, telling both Rundstedt and Rommel that they could not be deployed without his personal authorization. Two things were clear. The Allies would enjoy total air superiority, and the Germans could not look to the Kriegsmarine to attack the invasion fleet in the English Channel.

THE 'LONGEST DAY'

Despite the fact that, since the late summer of 1942, the Germans had been constructing the so-called Atlantic Wall, Rommel had a low opinion of it. He would defeat the invasion, he told his staff officers, on the beaches. The first 24 hours of the battle would be crucial. 'For us and for the Allies', he concluded, 'it will be the longest day'. As June dawned, German intelligence warned that the invasion was imminent. Then the weather broke. Rommel thought an invasion so unlikely that on the morning of 5 June, he went on leave to Germany to celebrate his wife's birthday. Early the next morning, Eisenhower struck, taking advantage of a 'window' in the unfavourable weather. The Germans were taken by surprise.

BATTLE FOR THE BEACHES

Over 9,000 Allied aircraft flew sorties against targets on or behind the beaches, dropping some 9,072 tonnes (10,000 tons) of bombs. The French Resistance joined in. At 2.00 am, the airborne divisions were dropped on their targets; at 6.30 am, after a protracted naval bombardment, the first waves of the main force stormed ashore.

On Utah, the US 4th Division was the first to land. It suffered only light casualties. On Omaha, the US 29th and 1st divisions ran into heavy opposition from the start. By 9 am, the beach was littered with bodies. The Americans eventually rallied and drove the Germans back from the bluffs dominating the beach.

The British and Canadians found the going easier and started to push rapidly inland. The British 3rd Division was halted 5 km (3 miles) short of Caen by a network of German defences that had been thrown up along a dominant ridge.

Nevertheless, by nightfall the Allied forces had secured their bridgeheads. Just as Rommel had feared, the Germans had lost their chance to drive the Allies back into the sea.

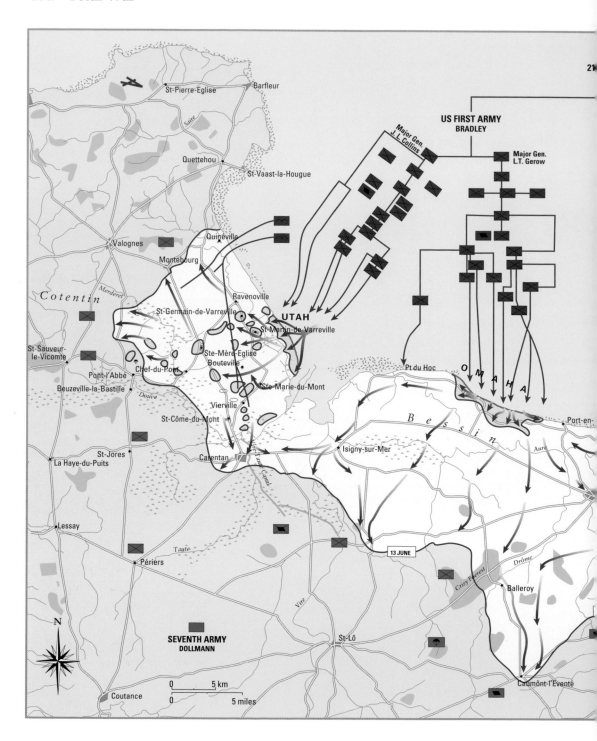

St-Pierre-Eglise
Barfleur
Saire
Quettehou
St-Vaast-la-Hougue

US FIRST ARMY
BRADLEY

Major Gen.
J. L. Collins

Major Gen.
L.T. Gerow

Valognes
Quinéville
Montebourg
Merderet
C o t e n t i n
Ravenoville
St-Germain-de-Varreville
UTAH
St-Martin-de-Varreville
St-Sauveur-
le-Vicomte
Ste-Mère-Eglise
Bouteville
Pont-l'Abbé
Chef-du-Pont
Pt du Hoc
O M A H A
Port-en-
Beuzeville-la-Bastille
Douve
Ste-Marie-du-Mont
Vierville
B e s s i n
St-Côme-du-Mont
Aure
St-Jores
La Haye-du-Puits
Carentan
Isigny-sur-Mer
Lessay
13 JUNE
Taute
Crisy Forest
Drôme
Ballerou
Périers
Vire
N
St-Lô
SEVENTH ARMY
DOLLMANN
Caumônt-l'Eventé
Coutance

0   5 km
0   5 miles

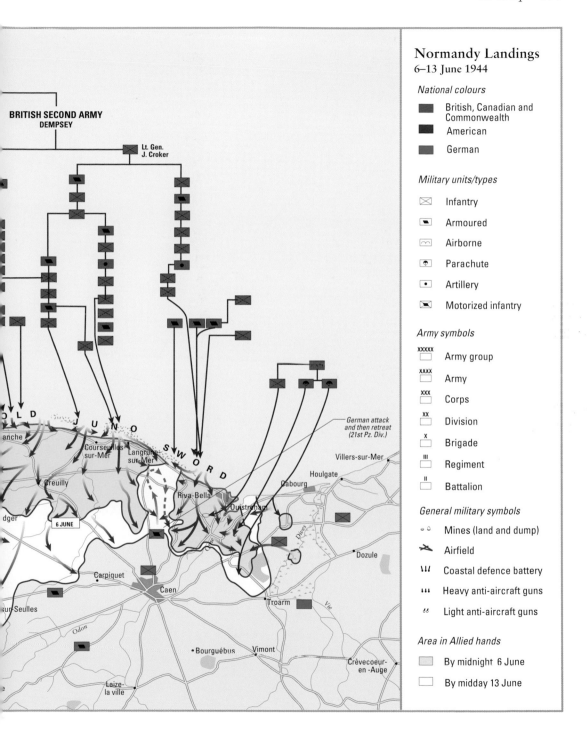

BRITISH SECOND ARMY
DEMPSEY

Lt. Gen.
J. Croker

German attack
and then retreat
(21st Pz. Div.)

anche

Courseulles-
sur-Mer

Langrune-
sur-Mer

Villers-sur-Mer

Creully

Cabourg

Houlgate

6 JUNE

Riva-Bella

Ouistreham

Dozule

Carpiquet

Caen

Troarm

Carpiquet

sur-Seulles

Odon

Bourguébus

Vimont

Crèvecoeur-
en-Auge

Laize-
la ville

Normandy Landings
6–13 June 1944

National colours

British, Canadian and
Commonwealth

American

German

Military units/types

Infantry

Armoured

Airborne

Parachute

Artillery

Motorized infantry

Army symbols

Army group

Army

Corps

Division

Brigade

Regiment

Battalion

General military symbols

Mines (land and dump)

Airfield

Coastal defence battery

Heavy anti-aircraft guns

Light anti-aircraft guns

Area in Allied hands

By midnight 6 June

By midday 13 June

Leyte Gulf

THE DEVASTATION OF ITS NAVY AND ITS FAILURE TO OUST THE ALLIES FROM LEYTE
WOULD MEAN THAT JAPAN WOULD LOSE ITS HOLD OVER THE PHILIPPINES, THUS
LOSING ITS SOURCES OF RAW MATERIALS AND OIL.

In autumn 1944, the United States decided that its next move in the Pacific war would be the liberation of the Philippines. The ground forces in the attack would be under the command of General Douglas MacArthur; to support him, Admiral Chester W. Nimitz assigned the US 7th Fleet commanded by Admiral Thomas Kinkaid and Admiral William 'Bull' Halsey's 3rd Fleet, together with Vice-Admiral Marc Mitscher's Fast Carrier Task Force.

Recognizing that losing the Philippines would mean that Japan was cut off from its sole remaining sources of war materials, the Japanese were prepared to risk everything to destroy the US invasion fleet. Their plan, devised by Admiral Soemu Toyoda, called for practically all of Japan's remaining naval strength to be thrown into battle.

Kurita, however, was far from beaten. Though he changed course, as if going to withdraw, under cover of darkness he resumed his westerly course...

TOYODA'S PLAN

Toyoda split his fleet into three separate task forces. Vice-Admiral Jisiburo Ozawa, with four aircraft carriers and a dozen other ships, would approach the Philippines from the north, acting as a decoy to draw off Halsey's fleet. Meanwhile, two powerful battleship squadrons would penetrate the central Philippines to converge on the invasion shipping in Leyte Gulf. The Southern Force, under the command of Vice-Admiral Shoji Nishimura, would sail via the Surigao Strait to the south of Leyte Gulf. The Centre Force, commanded by Vice-Admiral Takeo Kurita, would penetrate the San Bernadino Strait, sail down the coast of Samar and strike at the American invasion fleet from the north-east. Kurita had five battleships, ten heavy cruisers, two light cruisers and 15 destroyers at his disposal. Two of his battleships – the *Yamato* and *Musashi* – were the largest warships in the world at that time. The Japanese considered both of them to be unsinkable.

Battle started in the Sibuyan Sea on 23 October when two scouting US submarines sighted Kurita's Centre Force. They torpedoed and sank two heavy cruisers, including the *Atago*, Kurita's flagship, and severely damaged a third. The next day, waves of aircraft from Mitscher's carriers joined in the assault. Most of them concentrated on the *Musashi*. Having withstood almost constant air attacks for much of the day, the great, supposedly unsinkable battleship finally turned turtle and sank at 7.35 pm.

Kurita, however, was far from beaten. Though he changed course as if going to withdraw, under cover of darkness he resumed his westerly course. Believing him beaten, Halsey now ordered his entire fleet to sail north to engage Ozawa's carriers and their escorts. He left the San Bernadino Strait unguarded and Admiral Kincaid unsupported.

CRUSHING OF THE SOUTHERN FORCE

In the Surigao Strait, Kincaid was fighting his own battle. Warned that Nishimura's Southern Force was approaching, he ordered Rear-Admiral Jesse Oldendorf to intercept the Japanese before they could close for action. As Nishimura started to steam up the Surigao Strait that night, he was attacked by Oldendorf's waiting PT boats and then by his destroyers. As his ships emerged from the strait, he then found himself confronted by Oldendorf's battleships and cruisers. The resulting action was one-sided. Oldendorf's ships sank two Japanese battleships and a heavy cruiser. The rest of the Southern Force turned back to make its escape.

KURITA RETURNS

The battle was not over. As Oldendorf was concluding the action, he received the news that Kurita had returned to the attack. Debouching unopposed from the San Bernadino Strait, he had taken Kincaid's escort carrier squadron, commanded by Rear-Admiral Clifton Sprague, by surprise. They were all that stood between Kurita and the invasion beaches.

Sprague's carriers were not intended to withstand heavy fighting. The aircraft they carried were armed only for land operations. Nevertheless, given the situation, Sprague decided that he must fight a delaying action. While his carriers launched all their available aircraft and steamed towards the rest of 7th Fleet, he ordered his destroyers to attack. His aircraft, too, did what they could to slow down the Japanese attack.

Despite Sprague's gallantry, it looked as though Kurita was gaining the upper hand. Then, completely unexpectedly, he ordered his ships to break off the action and withdraw. Why he did this is uncertain. It may be that he feared Halsey was returning to the attack. Halsey, however, was far to the north, attacking Ozawa's carriers. At around 8.00 am, the first wave of Mitscher's aircraft attacked. The airstrikes continued until the evening, by which time all four carriers had been sunk or crippled beyond repair.

The action was not the total triumph for which Halsey had been hoping. Just as his surface ships were about to engage what remained of Ozawa's fleet, he was forced to break off the attack and steam south again to Kinkaid's assistance. In the event, Kurita had already withdrawn before Halsey's belated arrival.

The devastation of its navy and its failure to oust the Allies from Leyte would mean that Japan would lose its hold over the Philippines, thus losing its sources of raw materials and oil.

The Battle of Leyte Gulf and the Struggle for the Philippines
20–27 October 1944

➡ Japanese attacks

✈ Japanese air attack

⊕ Japanese airfield

➡ US attacks

✈ US air attack

⚓ Ship sunk

1 20 October: *US Sixth Army under General Krueger gains beachheads on the east coast of Leyte.*

2 23 October: *US submarines sink two Japanese cruisers and damage one. A US submarine sinks after running aground.*

3 24 October: *Southern Force 2 enters the Surigao Straits and is engaged by a US Navy detachment.*

4 24 October: *Southern Force 1 withdraws without entering the Surigao Straits.*

5 24 October: *USS* Princeton *sunk by Japanese shore-based aircraft.*

6 25 October: *Suspecting a trap, Kurita retreats back through the San Bernadino Strait.*

7 25 October: *Battle of Cape Engano, Northern Fleet engaged.*

The map shows the movements made by the Japanese and by the US during the Battle of Leyte Gulf.

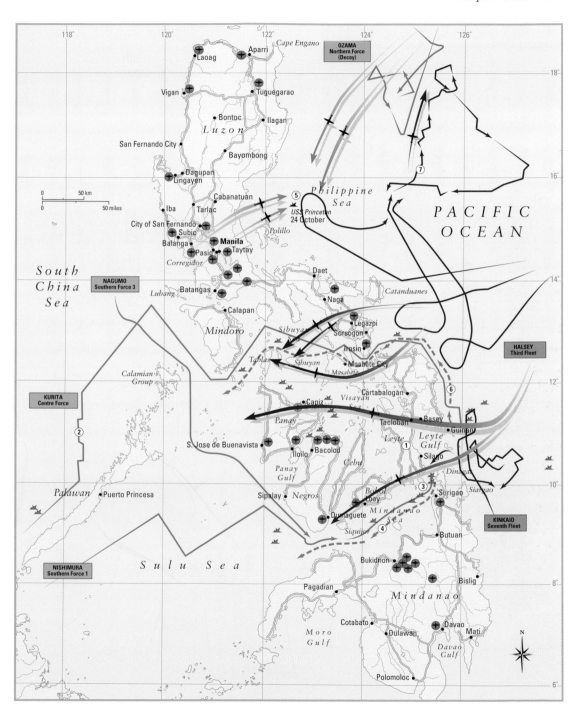

The Modern World

Since 1945, warfare has changed
significantly. With the advent of
nuclear weapons, the era of total war
came to an end. Localized conflicts
and guerrilla campaigns have
become the order of the day.

Inchon

WHEN US GENERAL DOUGLAS MACARTHUR PROPOSED LANDING UN TROOPS AT INCHON DURING THE KOREAN WAR, MANY OPPOSED HIM. UNDAUNTED, HE WENT AHEAD, FORCING HIS COMMUNIST OPPONENTS BACK INTO THEIR OWN COUNTRY.

When troops from communist North Korea crossed the 38th parallel into South Korea in June 1950, the United Nations (UN) rapidly took action. By nine votes to nil, the UN Security Council condemned North Korean aggression and authorized a peace-keeping force to be despatched to support the South Koreans in their struggle to maintain independence. Russia was boycotting Security Council meetings in protest at its members' refusal to grant communist China diplomatic recognition, so it could not veto the resolution.

The South Koreans were quickly in deep trouble. The massive North Korean invasion had caught them unawares and unprepared. Their army was speedily forced back to Pusan in the south-eastern corner of the Korean peninsula.

Communist victory seemed assured, but General Douglas MacArthur, the flamboyant commander of the largely American forces the UN had authorized to be sent to prop up the South Korean regime, had other ideas. While US troops, hastily despatched from occupation duties in Japan, formed a defensive ring around Pusan, he advocated launching a daring amphibious counter-strike.

MacArthur's plan was to land UN forces at Inchon, a port on the west coast not far from Seoul, South Korea's now-occupied capital. If successful, the North Koreans at Pusan would be outflanked and open to counter-attack. It would also sever their already-overstretched supply lines, thus forcing them to retreat.

The map shows the movements made by the UN in order to counter-attack the North Koreans in September–November 1950.

Korea–United Nations Counter-attack
15 September–25 November 1950

→ UN counter-attack   ▨ Pusan perimeter

— Front line with date

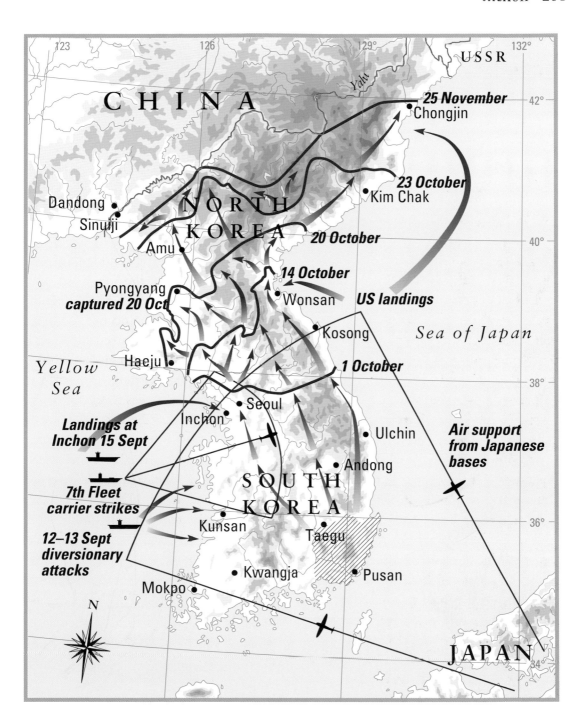

USSR

CHINA

25 November
Chongjin

NORTH
KOREA

23 October
Kim Chak

Dandong

Sinuiji

20 October

Amu

14 October

Pyongyang
captured 20 Oct

Wonsan

US landings

Kosong

Sea of Japan

*Yellow
Sea*

Haeju

1 October

Seoul

Inchon

**Landings at
Inchon 15 Sept**

Ulchin

**Air support
from Japanese
bases**

Andong

**7th Fleet
carrier strikes**

SOUTH
KOREA

*12–13 Sept
diversionary
attacks*

Kunsan

Taegu

Kwangja

Pusan

Mokpo

N

JAPAN

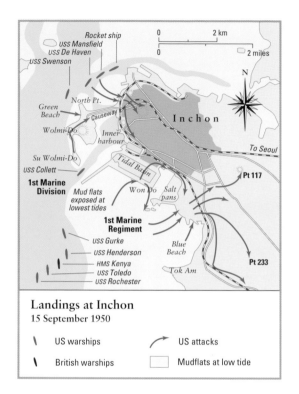

Landings at Inchon
15 September 1950

\   US warships   ⟶   US attacks

\   British warships   ▢   Mudflats at low tide

The map shows the landings of US troops at Inchon in September 1950, plus their supporting naval forces.

PLANNING THE LANDING

Preparing the plan started at the end of June, but it took nearly until the end of August to complete. The problems involved were immense. One of MacArthur's staff officers recalled how 'we drew up a list of every conceivable natural and geographical handicap and Inchon had them all'.

The harbour could be approached only via one long narrow channel – the so-called Flying Fish Channel. UN ships would have to twist and turn their way through it while battling its formidable currents. Inchon itself lacked beaches – at least in the conventional sense. It was surrounded by easily defended walls of natural rock. In addition, the North Koreans had installed artillery on the small island of Wolmi-do in the centre of the harbour.

Nevertheless, MacArthur pressed ahead. By the beginning of September, he had bulldozed Washington into giving permission for the attack to proceed. The landing was to take place on 15 September, when the tides would be high enough to allow his ships to navigate the approach channel. MacArthur chose the US Marines to lead the assault.

THE MARINES STRIKE

The invasion force sailed from Japan on 5 September. Despite encountering a fierce tropical storm, it made good progress, arriving off Inchon on schedule, As it neared the Flying Fish Channel, UN cruisers and destroyers moved in to sweep the channel for mines and then to bombard the North Korean positions on the island of Wolmi-do. The North Korean commander there confidently assured his superiors that he could repel any subsequent attack.

The North Koreans were over-optimistic. At around 6.30 am, Battalion

Landing Team 3 of the 5th Marines went ashore, landing on Green Beach. By noon, they had managed to capture the whole island, suffering only 14 casualties in the process, after which they defended the causeway leading to the mainland while waiting for reinforcements to arrive.

The second and third waves of Marines landed on Red and Blue Beaches at 5.30 pm. The Marines on Red Beach, located just north of the Wolmi-do causeway, quickly scaled the sea wall and linked up with their comrades defending the causeway. Together, the two forces pressed on into Inchon. By midnight, they had taken the city. In the meantime, the 1st Marine Regiment, which had landed on Blue Beach to the south, was moving up to help to consolidate the UN position.

The landing had taken the North Korean high command totally by surprise, but as UN troops moved towards Seoul, the communist resistance hardened. The city was completely liberated by 30 September after fierce house-to-house and hand-to-hand fighting.

THE BATTLE'S AFTERMATH

In the meantime, General Walton H. Walker's 8th Army had broken the North Korean stranglehold on Pusan and was advancing north, driving the North Koreans in headlong retreat across the 38th Parallel. The ebullient MacArthur, disregarding China's warning that it would enter the war if UN troops reached the river Yalu, urged his men forwards. He told President Harry S. Truman that he intended to end the war by Christmas.

In late October, however, Chinese forces flooded into North Korea. They drove MacArthur's troops back over the border and south of Seoul, where the position was eventually stabilized. Though MacArthur had overreached himself, there was no doubting the fact that the Inchon landings had been a brilliant strategic success.

FACT FILE

Inchon

Date: September 1950

Location: Inchon, South Korea

Historical Context: Korean War (1950–1953)

States Involved: United Nations, South Korea; North Korea

Commanders and Leaders: General Douglas MacArthur. Oliver P. Smith, Edward M. Almond, Arthur Dewey Struble (USA); Paik In-Yeop, Shin Hyun-Joon (South Korea); Choi Yong-Kun, Wol Ki Chan, Kim Il-sung, Wan Yong (North Korea)

Outcome: Decisive UN victory

Dien Bien Phu

WHEN CRACK FRENCH PARATROOPS TOOK ON VIET MINH FORCES IN THE
INDOCHINA WAR, THEIR COMMANDERS EXPECTED TO WIN A DECISIVE VICTORY.
INSTEAD, THEY WERE FORCED TO SURRENDER AFTER A 55-DAY SIEGE.

The battle at Dien Bien Phu was the brainchild of Lieutenant-General Henri Navarre, the newly appointed commander-in-chief of France's forces in Indochina. When he arrived in the colony in May 1953, Navarre found that, despite the fact the French had been fighting the Communist Viet Minh since 1946, no long-term plan had ever been devised to bring about the defeat of General Vo Nguyan Giap's forces. The French had reacted to Giap's every move, handing the strategic initiative to the enemy.

Navarre refused to put up with this situation. He and his staff came up with the notion of setting up heavily fortified camps, known as 'hedgehogs', to interdict the key Viet Minh supply lines and so force Giap to pull back his forces. Dien Bien Phu, a village situated in a heart-shaped valley surrounded by thickly wooded hills close to the Laotian frontier, was chosen to be the focal point of the entire operation.

Navarre believed that it would act like a magnet, irresistibly attracting the Viet Minh and tempting the Vietnamese commander into finally fighting a setpiece battle that he could never win. The Viet Minh would supposedly be ground down remorselessly by superior French fire power and the war would be over.

Though the French knew that five of Giap's divisions were converging on the valley, they refused to accept that he could muster sufficient strength... to overwhelm their positions.

SETTING THE TRAP

The operation began on 20 November 1953, when wave after wave of French paratroops were dropped in and around the village. Commanded by Colonel Christian de Castries, they quickly consolidated their drop zones and crushed local Viet Minh opposition. They then busied themselves building a chain of eight fortified strong points protecting a central airstrip. As there were no passable roads in the area, the paratroopers were totally dependent on air support to supply them. Over the coming weeks, Castries' force swelled as more men, artillery and light tanks were flown in to reinforce him.

Huguette, Claudine, Eliane and Dominique were in the centre of the valley. Gabrielle, Anne-Marie and Beatrice were positioned to the north, north-west and north-east. Isabelle, slightly to the south, protected the garrison's auxiliary airstrip. Apparently, they were all named after Castries' various mistresses. On paper, the positions seemed formidable, but they had an intrinsic weakness. The French had made no attempt to fortify the surrounding hills, partly because of supply difficulties, but mainly because

they completely underestimated the Viet Minh's offensive capabilities. Though they knew that five of Giap's divisions were converging on the valley, they stubbornly

The map shows the positioning of the Vietnamese infantry at the Battle of Dien Bien Phu.

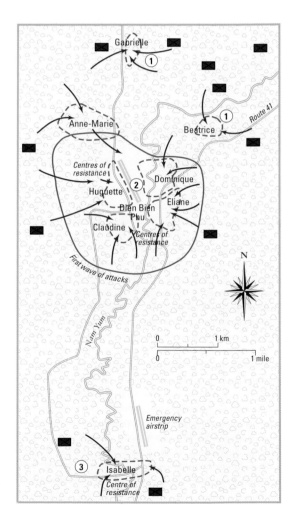

Battle of Dien Bien Phu
March–May 1954

■ Vietnamese Infantry

(1) The first wave of Viet Minh attacks takes out the outer defences of the French-held airfield.

(2) The second wave causes the French to withdraw into a smaller perimeter in which they can only be resupplied from the air.

(3) A third attack takes the outpost to the south; the French capitulate soon after.

The remnants of artillery from the conflict between the Viet Minh and the French are still found scattered across the country.

refused to accept that he could muster sufficient strength, particularly in artillery, to overwhelm their positions. They were soon to be disillusioned.

FROM BATTLE TO SIEGE

Recognizing the French Achilles heel, Giap moved around 50,000 Viet Minh troops into the surrounding hills, together with most of his heavy artillery and anti-aircraft guns. His plan was to isolate and destroy the outlying strong points before launching

an all-out assault on the central positions. He started shelling the French towards the end of January 1954; by March, he was ready to attack.

At 5.00 pm on 13 March, the Viet Minh began their assault – first on Beatrice and then on Gabrielle. After bitter fighting under the light of a full moon, Beatrice fell. Gabrielle held out a little longer, but the French were eventually forced to abandon the position, which was now effectively outflanked. Giap quickly moved his men to the north-west to capture Anne-Marie. With all three of these strong points safely in his hands, his mortars were within range of the vital main French airstrip. They opened fire, forcing its closure.

The consequences of closing the airstrip were catastrophic. From then on, the only way the beleaguered French garrison could be reinforced and resupplied was by parachute drop and Giap's anti-aircraft guns made this kind of operation extremely precarious. Nor could the French evacuate their wounded. With ammunition, medical supplies and food running short, conditions within the remaining positions deteriorated rapidly.

THE FRENCH SURRENDER

Castries' troops were still putting up a spirited resistance. After the failure of assaults on Dominique, Huguette and Isabelle, Giap was forced to reconsider his plan. On 5 April, he ordered his engineers to start constructing an elaborate system of trenches, which slowly but surely began inching nearer and nearer to the French lines. By this time, the French had pulled back to a new defensive zone just under 1.5 km (1 mile) in diameter where they planned to make their last stand.

On 1 May, the Viet Minh launched its last ferocious assault. Soaked through by the monsoon, which had broken a few days previously, and, in many instances, now totally demoralized, the French paratroops did not fight to the last man. On 7 May, recognizing the fact that their position was hopeless, Castries and 11,000 of his soldiers surrendered. The garrison at Isabelle capitulated 24 hours later.

FACT FILE

Dien Bien Phu

Date: March–May 1954

Location: Dien Bien Phu, Vietnam

Historical Context: First Indochina War (1946–1954)

Forces Involved: Viet Minh; French

Commanders and Leaders: Christian de Castries, Pierre Langlais (France); Vo Nguyan Giap (Viet Minh)

Outcome: Decisive Viet Minh victory

The Six-Day War

WHEN ISRAEL RESPONDED TO ARAB PROVOCATION BY ATTACKING EGYPT, JORDAN AND SYRIA IN JUNE 1967, IT TOOK THE ISRAELIS ONLY SIX DAYS TO SMASH THE ARAB FORCES CONFRONTING THEM AND WIN AN OUTRIGHT VICTORY.

The Six-Day War with Egypt began shortly after dawn on 5 June, when the Israeli Air Force wiped out the Egyptian Air Force on the ground in a devastating series of attacks on its main air bases. More than 200 Egyptian aircraft were caught on the ground and destroyed, while the Israelis lost only 19 aeroplanes. Meanwhile, three Israeli armoured columns pressed forwards into the Sinai Desert and the Gaza Strip, ready to take on the huge Egyptian forces that had been massing there for weeks. These totalled almost 100,000 men, backed up by 1,000 tanks and abundant artillery. The Israelis, on the other hand, faced with fighting a war on three fronts, could put only 45,000 troops and 700 tanks into the field.

On the ground, the Israeli assault began at 8.00 am that morning, when leading elements of the division commanded by Israel Tal advanced in the north towards the Egyptian stronghold at Rafah. The plan was for them to isolate the Gaza Strip and then move westwards through El Arish. Tal hoped for a quick breakthrough, but instead his armour encountered tough opposition. It was not until one of his tank battalions advanced towards Rafah 'regardless of cost' with a parachute brigade swinging west through the desert in support that the deadlock was broken. As Tal pushed towards the Suez Canal, the Egyptian forces opposing him were destroyed, dispersed or taken prisoner.

In the centre, Ariel Sharon's division met with equal success, while to the

With Egypt and Jordan defeated, the Israelis were left facing Syria. The latter believed that its position on the Golan Heights was impregnable. It was wrong.

The map shows the movements made by the Arab and Israeli forces during the Six-Day War.

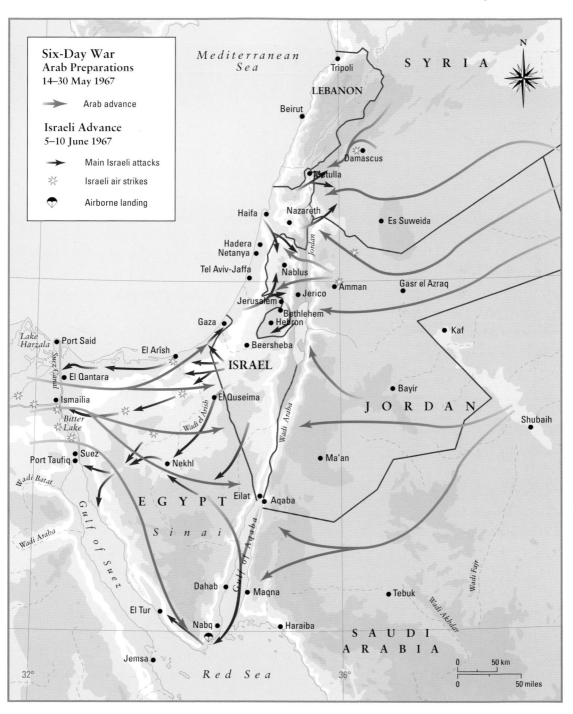

Six-Day War
Arab Preparations
14–30 May 1967

→ Arab advance

Israeli Advance
5–10 June 1967

→ Main Israeli attacks

✳ Israeli air strikes

Airborne landing

Mediterranean Sea

SYRIA

Tripoli

LEBANON

Beirut

Damascus

Metulla

Haifa

Nazareth

Es Suweida

Hadera

Netanya

Tel Aviv-Jaffa

Nablus

Jordan

Amman

Gasr el Azraq

Jerusalem

Jerico

Bethlehem

Hebron

Gaza

Kaf

El Arîsh

Beersheba

ISRAEL

El Qantara

Bayir

Ismailia

El Quseima

JORDAN

Port Said

Lake Harzala

Suez Canal

Wadi el Arîsh

Shubaih

Bitter Lake

Port Taufiq

Suez

Nekhl

Ma'an

Wadi Batat

Wadi Araba

Gulf of Suez

EGYPT

Eilat

Aqaba

Sinai

Gulf of Aqaba

Wadi Araba

Dahab

Maqna

Tebuk

Wadi Fajr

El Tur

Nabq

Haraiba

Wadi Akhdar

SAUDI ARABIA

Jemsa

Red Sea

32°

36°

0   50 km

0   50 miles

N

The Zion Gate in the southern wall of Jerusalem's Old City. The gate still bears the bullet scars from the Six-Day War in 1967.

hammered unmercifully from the sky by Israeli jets. This only reinforced the panic. On 9 June, a ceasefire came into effect. It was the end of the battle.

WAR ON THE WEST BANK

The campaign on the West Bank of the river Jordan started when Jordanian aeroplanes began raiding Israeli air bases while Arab Legion troops crossed the armistice line in Jerusalem to attack the Israeli enclaves in the southern part of the city. Israel's response was immediate and deadly. Its air force caught Jordan's jets on the ground refuelling and destroyed all of them, while units from Uzi Narkiss' Central Command started to advance towards Nablus and Jerusalem. In the latter instance, the priorities were to link up with the Jewish enclaves and to secure the high ground to the north of the city.

Colonel Uri Ben-Ari's 10th Mechanized Brigade led the attack, suddenly turning off the road from Tel Aviv to Jerusalem to attack the Jordanian positions on the Ramallah Ridge. By midnight on 5 June, it had captured Radar Hill, Abdul Aziz and Beit Iksa, the three heights dominating the roads to the north and east of the city. Colonel Mordechai Gur's 55th Parachute Brigade then advanced on Jerusalem itself.

Gur faced a formidable task, since the Jordanians had created an elaborate

north Abraham Yoffe's troops succeeded in blocking the eastern end of the Mitla Pass, close to the Suez Canal. This put an end to Egyptian hopes of conducting any orderly withdrawal. On 7 and 8 June, as the Israeli advance continued, many Egyptian units broke and fled, abandoning their equipment as they streamed back towards the canal in search of safety. They were confronted by Yoffe's tanks and were defensive position to cement their hold on the Old City. His paratroopers, however, were tough, seasoned fighters. When their attack began the following day, they resolutely inched their way forwards, clearing each Jordanian position in turn. They won control of most of the Sheik Jarrach district, captured Ammunition Hill and pushed on as far as the Rockefeller Museum before entering the Old City itself. By 10.00 am, they had got as far as the Wailing Wall. Shortly after that, with the entire Old City now under Israeli control, both sides agreed to a ceasefire.

STORMING THE GOLAN HEIGHTS

With Egypt and Jordan defeated, the Israelis were left facing the Syrians. The latter believed that their positions on the Golan Heights were impregnable. They were wrong. On 9 June, after three hours of intense bombing, Israelis forces commanded by David Elazar crossed the border. He launched five attacks, the key one being in the north where the Syrians least expected it. Though suffering heavy casualties, his armour and infantry broke through the Syrian defences. Reinforced by a fresh armoured brigade, the advancing Israelis prepared for a multi-pronged attack on the key town of Quneitra.

Damascus radio prematurely announced that the town had fallen – probably to try to provoke Russian intervention. The ploy backfired. Believing that Quneitra had been captured, Syrian troops throughout the Golan panicked and fled. By nightfall, all resistance had collapsed. The Six-Day War was over. Against the odds, Israel had succeeded in turning back the tide of a huge multi-nation offensive operation.

FACT FILE
The Six-Day War

Date: 5–10 June 1967

Location: Middle East

Historical Context: A result of hostile relations between Arabs and Israel

States Involved: Israel; Egypt, Jordan, Syria

Commanders and Leaders: Moshe Dayan, Mordechai Gur, Uzi Narkiss, Israel Tal, Yitzhak Rabin, Ariel Sharon, Ezer Weizman, Yeshayahu Gavish, Mordechai Hod (Israel); Abdel Hakim Amer, Abdul Manim Riad (Egypt); Zaid ibn Shaker, Asad Ghanma (Jordan); Nureddin al-Atassi, Abdul Rahman Arif (Syria)

Outcome: Decisive Israeli victory

The Gulf War

WHEN IRAQ INVADED KUWAIT IN 1990, A UN COALITION CAME TO THE COUNTRY'S RESCUE. IT WAS THE FIRST TIME IN HISTORY THAT AIR POWER PROVED TO BE THE MOST IMPORTANT FACTOR IN DETERMINING THE OUTCOME OF A WAR.

In August 1990, Iraq triggered the events that were to lead to the Gulf War by sending troops into Kuwait, its tiny southern neighbour. The exact reasons why Iraqi dictator Saddam Hussein decided to attack still remain unclear; he himself used the excuse that Kuwait was 'stealing' Iraqi oil from the oilfields close to the two countries' frontier.

On 2 August, 100,000 Iraqi troops, spearheaded by three divisions of the elite Republican Guard, powered into Kuwait, heading for Kuwait City and the Saudi Arabian border. Though the Kuwaitis had been aware of the Iraqi build-up, their resistance was minimal. In just four-and-a-half hours, the Republican Guard reached the outskirts of the capital; airborne Iraqi Special Forces were already in action inside the city. Within a day, the entire country was under Iraqi control. Saddam proclaimed that Kuwait was now part of Iraq. He sent in reinforcements and waited to see how the outside world would react.

FORGING THE COALITION

US President George Bush was determined to oppose Iraq. When King Fahd appealed to him to send aid to protect Saudi Arabia against potential attack, he responded immediately. He ordered crack US ground and air forces to be deployed on Saudi soil, while the US 6th Fleet was also despatched to the Gulf to provide further support. General H. 'Stormin' Norman Schwarzkopf was sent to Saudi Arabia to take command. The Americans called the operation 'Desert Shield'.

The United States was not alone in coming to Saudi Arabia's assistance. Following Iraq's condemnation by the United Nations (UN), a multi-

Iraqi radar was savaged by helicopters and their airfields were blitzed mercilessly; bombers and Cruise missiles wreaked havoc wherever they struck...

national coalition was rapidly organized. Contingents from Britain, France, Italy, Belgium, the Netherlands, Canada, Egypt, Syria, Bahrain, Oman and Qatar joined the Saudis and Americans in preparing to resist any further Iraqi attempt at aggression. Gradually, the coalition forces built up their strength. Eventually, more than 500,000 troops were to be involved.

OPERATION 'DESERT STORM'

The Gulf War proper started on 16 January 1991, the day after the UN deadline for Saddam to withdraw from Kuwait expired. The coalition launched an all-out air assault, striking at Iraqi positions in Kuwait, their long supply and communication lines back to their home bases and key targets inside Iraq. The attack's awesome magnitude was unprecedented. Iraqi radar installations were savaged by helicopters and their airfields were blitzed mercilessly; bombers and Tomahawk cruise missiles wreaked havoc wherever they struck. Even Baghdad was not immune from attack, though a special mission targeting Saddam personally failed in its objective.

With their air defences neutralized, the Iraqis had no real means of defence against the onslaught. The one air raid

Operation Desert Storm began with a massive air offensive that gave way to ground attacks in the second stage.

they managed to launch against a Saudi oil refinery was a dismal failure, though they did manage to fire a few Scud missiles at Saudi Arabia and Israel. Saddam therefore resorted to using hostages as human shields for prime coalition targets.

The coalition pounded the hapless Iraqis in Kuwait and southern Iraq with fuel and cluster bombs, armour-piercing smart bombs and a barrage of missiles. By the time Schwarzkopf was ready to launch his ground attack, few of Saddam's troops were in a fit state to fight. The majority were totally demoralized. Schwarzkopf's

FACT FILE
The Gulf War

Dates: 1990–1991

Location: Iraq, Kuwait, Israel, Saudi Arabia

States Involved: Iraq; UN coalition forces, Kuwait, Saudi Arabia, Israel (non-belligerent)

Key Commanders: Norman Schwarzkopf, John A. Warden III, Colin Powell, Charles Horner, Calvin Waller, Frederick Franks (United States); Ali Hassan al-Majid, Salah Aboud Mahmoud (Iraq)

Outcome: Decisive UN victory

Aftermath: The UN victory altered the balance of power in the region by decisively weakening Iraq.

plan was to keep the Iraqi front-line forces pinned down, while his highly mobile armour swung around in a left hook to outflank and encircle the enemy, cutting their supply lines and putting an end to all hopes of an orderly withdrawal.

The ground assault started on 24 February. The US Marines led the way, thrusting into the heart of the Iraqi forces in central Kuwait. The Arab participants moved up the coast, while the US 18th Airborne Corps and the French 6th Armoured Division stormed into action on the left. The US 7th Corps, the 24th Infantry Division and the British 1st Armoured Division swiftly followed up the initial attack.

THE 'HIGHWAY OF DEATH'

As the coalition forces moved inexorably onwards, the Iraqis panicked. Many surrendered on the spot. Others tried to flee down the one road left open to them – the highway leading from Kuwait City to the Al Jahra Pass. The road soon became jammed with hundreds of vehicles laden with Iraqi loot. It was then that the coalition bombers struck. Thousands of Iraqis were killed or wounded.

As Schwarzkopf's forces moved to sever this last avenue of retreat, President Bush brought the campaign to an end, ordering the cessation of all offensive military operations. This allowed the remaining Iraqi forces to make their escape and return to Iraq. Nevertheless, the facts spoke for themselves. The humiliated Saddam had lost what he had christened 'the mother of all battles'. However, as history tells, it was not the end of Saddam and his aggression towards the West and his own people. Many critics in the West were dismayed that Saddam had not been toppled when the opportunity presented itself in 1991.

The map shows the movements made by the Iraqi forces and the Allied forces during the Gulf War.

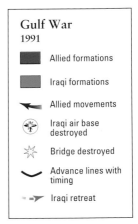

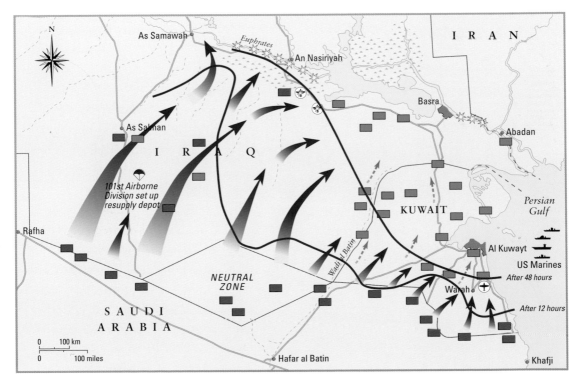

Fall of Baghdad

WHEN US-LED COALITION FORCES WENT TO WAR AGAIN WITH IRAQ IN 2003, IT TOOK THEM LESS THAN 40 DAYS TO CRUSH IRAQI MILITARY RESISTANCE, CAPTURE BAGHDAD AND FINALLY TOPPLE SADDAM HUSSEIN FROM POWER.

Operation 'Iraqi Freedom', the full-scale invasion of Iraq by Coalition forces, began on 19 March 2003. Taking the decision to launch it, US President George W. Bush claimed that Saddam Hussein's regime was flouting UN sanctions, was sponsoring terrorist groups and was still developing nuclear, biological and chemical weapons of mass destruction.

World opinion, however, was not as in favour of military intervention as it had been at the time of the Gulf War. Despite protests and mass demonstrations around the world, the US and British governments decided to act, even without full Security Council authorization. On 17 March, Bush issued an ultimatum to Saddam, giving him and his sons 48 hours to leave the country. If they refused, war would result.

On 17 March, Bush issued an ultimatum to Saddam, giving him and his sons 48 hours to leave the country. If they refused, war would result.

PREPARING TO ATTACK

US General Tommy Franks was in command of the Coalition forces, which were massed in staging areas close to the border between Kuwait and Iraq. The general had more than 260,000 troops ready for action. Some 214,000 of them were American and 45,000 were British. The balance consisted of a few small contingents from several other countries.

Compared with the Coalition forces, the Iraqis opposing them were ill-equipped and under-trained. Nevertheless, there were many more of them. Coalition intelligence estimated that its troops would face more than 400,000 Iraqis, the majority of whom were regular conscripts. Iraq also had 44,000 Fedayeen Saddam troops available, plus up to 650,000 troops in reserve.

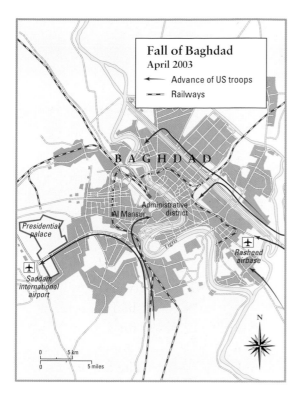

The map shows US troops advancing into Baghdad, eventually causing the city to fall.

The Iraqis expected Franks to adopt the same strategy as before, but he had the opposite in mind. The air attack would be short and sharp, after which his troops would move immediately into the attack. The plan was for some of them to secure key positions in southern Iraq, while the others, bypassing heavily populated areas where the Fedayeen were expected to be strongest, would advance rapidly north-west up the Tigris and Euphrates river valleys and make straight for Baghdad.

Capturing the Iraqi capital, Franks believed, would inevitably bring about the collapse of Saddam's regime.

THE ADVANCE BEGINS

The Coalition air forces struck early in the morning of 20 March. US stealth bombers dropped smart bombs on a bunker complex in the heart of Baghdad, hoping to kill Saddam, who was believed to be meeting there with the rest of the Iraqi leadership. The strike failed in its objective, but Coalition aircraft and Tomahawk cruise missiles targeted other government buildings, military installations and command centres in the city successfully. Shortly afterwards, the Coalition land forces surged across the Iraqi frontier.

The attack got off to a good start. By the end of the day, British troops operating in the south had stormed and secured the port of Umm Qasr and the Al Faw Peninsula had been occupied. The 7th Armoured Brigade was pressing forwards towards Basra, Iraq's second-largest city. The British force reached its outskirts the next day.

Meanwhile, the US 1st Marine Division had secured the Rumaila oilfields before turning towards An Nasiriyah. There, the Americans received their first check. The 2nd Marine Expeditionary Brigade, which had been tasked with securing the town

Saddam Hussein at his trial lectures the court; he was condemned and eventually executed by the new Iraqi regime.

and its vital bridges across the Euphrates, was forced to come to the rescue of the 507th Maintenance Company, which had been ambushed by the Fedayeen. Fighting continued until the end of March. In the south, the British were still battling to capture Basra. They did not gain control of the entire city until 6 April.

BATTLE FOR BAGHDAD

As US forces advanced towards Baghdad, they came up against resistance from the four divisions of the Republican Guard that had been deployed to defend the city. Fierce fighting, over-extended supply lines and, to cap it all, a violent sandstorm slowed the Coalition advance down to a crawl. Eventually, the Americans paused 96 km (60 miles) short of their goal.

The attack resumed on 4 April. As the Iraqis weakened, the advancing Americans succeeded in winning control of Saddam International airport before launching two 'thunder runs' into the capital. The first was a reconnaissance in force; the second, on 7 April, succeeded in penetrating the heart of the administrative quarter. Meanwhile, other American forces were closing in on the city. On 9 April, all Iraqi resistance collapsed.

There was no sign of Saddam. He and other Iraqi leaders had fled. Tikrit, his home town, fell on 14 April; the northern

FACT FILE
Fall of Baghdad

Date: March–May 2003

Location: Iraq

States Involved: Iraq; US-led coalition forces

Leaders: Saddam Hussein (Iraq); George W. Bush (United States)

Outcome: Decisive Coalition victory

Aftermath: The coalition occupied Iraq for many years afterwards, though its forces met with increasing guerrilla resistance.

Invasion of Iraq
21 March–9 April 2003

Main axis of advance
with date

Supporting axis of
advance with date

Securing line of
communications with
date

cities of Kirkuk and Mosul had already
been liberated by Kurdish freedom fighters,
backed by US Special Forces who had been
parachuted into the region. On 1 May,
President Bush, speaking on the flight
deck of the aircraft carrier USS *Abraham*

*The map shows the invasion of Iraq by US-led coalition forces, which
resulted in the fall of Saddam and the capture of Baghdad.*

Lincoln, declared the war to be at an end.
The question now was how peace could be
best restored.

Index

Acknowledgements

We would like to thank the following for the use of their pictures reproduced in this book:

AFP
180

Corbis
139, 143, 148

Getty Images
218

Shutterstock
18, 21, 22, 26, 32, 36, 41, 45, 50, 54, 58, 61, 66, 72, 76, 78, 80, 84, 88, 92, 96, 99, 104, 109, 114, 118, 122, 131, 132, 134, 137, 144, 155, 156, 160, 163, 167, 206, 210, 213

All other photographs and illustrations are the copyright of Quantum Publishing. While every effort has been made to credit contributors, the publisher would like to apologise should there have been any omissions or errors – and would be pleased to make the appropriate correction for future editions of the book.